BORN FOR THIS

JOSHUA DILLARD

BORN FOR THIS

BOLDLY BECOME WHO YOU WERE BORN TO BE

Shrewd Publishing House

CONTENTS

CONTENTS

To every situation that helped mold me into the person I am today, good or bad, beautiful or ugly, Thank You.

- Joshua

WHAT HAPPENED TO YOUR WONDER

Do you remember? Do you remember being told as a kid that anything you put your mind to was possible, that if you believe it you can achieve it. Do you remember taking risks without worry? Do you remember how inquisitive and curious you were, how full of adventure you used to be? Have you ever stopped to ask yourself what happened?

As a child, I can remember being full of freedom, hope, and optimism. I didn't have many worries then; the only thing I had to worry about was trying not to disturb my 3rd grade class by being the class clown. My mom shut that down pretty quickly when she showed up to my school unannounced one day. The teacher had called and told her that she was having problems with me. I guess my mom had to see it with her own eyes. When I turned around and caught her piercing eyes looking at me through the glass on the door, my heart must have fallen into my stomach. I knew I was in trouble. According to my mom, I wasn't a bad child, but I was having the time of my life in class that day. I knew the consequences were soon to come as my mom walked into the class to greet the teacher while looking at me and mouthing "I'm going to get you". I just knew that if I straightened up, her anger would have subsided and she would have forgotten about the whole thing by the time she made it home that day. But I must admit, those were the days.

I know you're probably thinking to yourself, "How"? Well, in those days you didn't have to worry much about the consequences of your actions. I mean, sure, you would get in trouble, but for the most part after a quick punishment, you moved on with your life and went back to playing with your favorite toy. You didn't have many responsibilities and the expectations of people didn't weigh you down. You were a kid, a kid with an imagination and you could go wherever that imagination would take you.

For example, I remember one of my favorite television shows as a kid was Rugrats. These kids were a group of friends who were so full of life and adventure. They would find themselves getting into things that were dangerous and would somehow always make it out ok. Of course, as a kid I'm not taking into consideration that this is a carefully crafted fiction story. For all I know, these kids are real and these adventures are real, and I wanted to go on an adventure of my own. The only thing I could see is how much fun they were having. If they made it out ok, so would I.

I remember watching one episode where Susie and Angelica had a pretty intense race. Susie was on her big wheel and Angelica was in her fire truck. My brother and I had our eyes glued to the television in awe of how much fun they were having, and that's when it happened. We looked at each other, glanced over at our big wheels, and came up with our master plan....Cue the Mission Impossible music!

We decided we wanted to up-the-stakes, so we conspired against our uncle who was babysitting us at the time. He didn't stand a chance. Our mission was simple: slip out of our uncle's 2-bedroom apartment located on the second floor, and go get some candy located at the nearest convenience store. Getting out of the apartment would be the easiest part, since our uncle was often too focused on the latest basketball game to notice we were gone. But the hardest part would be getting down the stairs. Honestly, I can't even tell you how we made it down the stairs, I just know that we did. We were determined.

From there, we mounted our big wheels and peddled towards the nearest grocery store while cars blew their horns as they passed by. The sheer wind from those cars almost knocked us off of our tiny big wheels, but we peddled like our lives depended on it, which quite frankly, it did. We finally made it to the grocery store, parked our big wheels, and walked in. Once we saw the candy we came in there for, we grabbed it and commenced to walk out of the store. That's when some sweaty guy with a badge grabbed our arms at the door and said, "Hey, where are your parents?! You have to pay for that!" Parents? Pay? Who needs money when you have adventure?!

Unfortunately, adventure didn't quite cover the tab of these two lost kids of what seemed to be irresponsible parents. We didn't quite think our master plan through. We thought that we wouldn't be recognized as 6 and 7-year olds, and didn't take into consideration that we actually needed money to pay for our candy. Wow, so that's what our parents were doing when they would check out at the register, paying for stuff. Who knew?

After they finally reached my mom by phone, she was furious. We could hear her and my uncle arguing in the next room for hours. She screamed, "Do you know that my babies could have been killed?! What if they would have fallen down the stairs?! What if they would have gotten hit by a car?! What if the CPS would have taken them away from me?!" Yeah sure, we got in a little trouble, but ultimately our actions weren't our responsibility because we were just kids. We didn't really understand the gravity of what we were doing. All we knew was the mission was accomplished. As we sat in front of the television safely at home eating starburst, I thought to myself, "Top that, Susie and Angelica!"

Why is it important that I share this story with you? Because as children, we weren't thinking about the potential danger we put ourselves in. We weren't concerned about the consequences of our actions and we weren't afraid to take risks. We were curious and had unexplainable, unconscionable confidence and optimism.

Now, I want you to think back on a time where you did something dangerous and stupid when you were a kid. I know you must have at least one moment or two, or three, or four. At that time, were you really considering the consequences of your actions? Did you think about all the things that could possibly happen because of your undeveloped decision? When we think of these moments, we often tend to label them as mistakes. We look at them with disdain because of how ignorant we were at the time. How in the world did we make such an incomprehensible decision?

Do you want to know what made you make that decision? Wonder.

You were gripped by adolescence and the curiosity of not knowing, but wanting to find out. You had admiration for the unfamiliar and inexplicable. You were astonished, excited, and amazed by the things you didn't quite understand yet. They didn't scare you. They filled you with awe as you marveled at the possibilities.

What happened to that feeling?

What happened to your wonder?

As a child developing in the womb of your mother, you don't know anything about the world you're about to be born into. You don't know that you will have disappointments; that the plans you make for your life will not go as planned, and that your losses will sometimes outweigh and outpace your wins.

Your dreams will eventually become fairytales of your past as you try to survive the reality of your present while barely holding on to the promise of your future. Unfortunately, you are not equipped with the realities of life when you are in the womb. And if you were fully aware of tragedies that life would bring, do you think that you would have opted in if you had the choice? I know many people wouldn't.

When you're born, all you know is that when you open your eyes for the first time, you're in a whole new world. I imagine that this could be a very scary experience for a baby which is probably why they cry. You're cold, seeing new things for the first time, hearing new sounds, and just trying to make out what the heck is going on. You're looking around, barely able to open your eyes, and trying to make sense of everything happening around you outside of the womb. The voice of your mother sounds familiar but you can hear it more clearly now. You can feel and touch the cheeks of your father; so,this is what skin feels like.

I imagine that in this moment there are two emotions that a baby must be feeling: one is fear, the other is curiosity. As a newborn, you become more and more curious. The world is your oyster now. First, you could barely crawl, but you were so adamant to see what that little yellow thing making those sounds was, that you willed yourself into motion. You were curious. Even when you finally stood for the first time in your crib, your curiosity made you believe that "I could probably escape this crib if I tried hard enough." Regardless of the threat of possibly seriously hurting yourself, guess what? You were curious.

I asked you a question earlier and that question was, "What happened to your wonder?" The answer is actually quite simple: life. Life happened to your wonder.

See, wonder can be defined as a feeling of surprise mingled with admiration, caused by something beautiful, unexpected, unfamiliar, or inexplicable. But guess what, there's no way you can truly experience WONDER if this thing called living has sucked the "life" out of your curiosity. The reality is, without curiosity, you can never experience true wonder.

The reality is, without curiosity, you can never experience true wonder.

We, as adult human beings, fail to realize that we are not much different from newborn babies. The things that make us thrive, move forward, overcome obstacles, and achieve our deepest aspirations are often a combination of two emotions: fear and curiosity. The tragedy with adults that makes us lower than infants is that we choose to live the majority of our adulthood consumed by one emotion: fear, because our life experiences have suffocated our curiosity.

Ask yourself, when's the last time you acted on your curiosity? There's a caveat here before you answer this question because anyone can be curious about a new dinner recipe, trying a new restaurant, or transferring to a new mobile provider. That's not the type of curiosity that I'm referring to, because there's no imminent threat of danger with any of those examples that I mentioned above. It's easy to be curious about something when there's no imminent threat of danger. But if I asked you when's the last time you went skydiving, your response would probably be drastically different and not as casual. Why? Because there's an imminent threat of danger with skydiving. What's that? If the lever you pull to release the parachute does not open in time, it will result in your death.

As an infant, do you think you worried about breaking your arm or leg when you crawled out of that crib? Do you think you considered how much pain you would be in if you touched the scorching hot stove? No you didn't, even though all of those examples could result in serious consequences.

Now ask yourself another question: when was the last time you let fear, which can also be disguised as sensibility, stop you from doing something that you knew in your gut was the right thing to do?

I can guarantee that for most of you, the latter far outweighs the former.

As we become more experienced in life, our experience begins to chip away at our curiosity. We become less curious and more prudent, less inquisitive and more careful, less investigative and more leery. To sum it up, we take less risks, and risks are what fuel curiosity.

Curiosity is the breeding place for Wonder.

So the million dollar question is, how do you get your wonder back? Can it be reignited or is it a lost cause? Should you succumb to the predictable unenthusiastic day-to-day normal life that you've grown familiar with, or can you start over and become who you were born to be?

The most important thing that I really want you to believe is that who you were born to be is filled with wonder, awe, and amazement. It's not filled with fear alone, it's also filled with curiosity. The funny thing about all of this is that you probably think that you've reached your full potential, that there isn't anything else. But something deep down won't let you swallow that lie as the truth. If that were the case, you would not be reading this book.

Many books tell you that you need courage and bravery to overcome your fear. And to an extent, that's true. But what if I told you to think about how brave you could become if you just became curious. If you could find a way to tap into audacious curiosity, you would unlock all of the courage you could ever need.

HELD HOSTAGE BY THE
TRAUMA OF MY EXPERIENCES

Most times, we really can't comprehend how much the trauma of our experiences is holding us hostage. When we were born, we didn't have the agony of our experiences to pull from. Things were new. They were fresh and exciting. We were curious. But as we grew older, so did our skepticism and so did our doubt. Skepticism is the sister of fear. It grew with us, aged with us, and began slowly corroding the hearts of our imagination. As we grew older, like a stubborn cancer that rejected chemotherapy, our skepticism would not take this lying down and just die. No, it grew with us. And the more the realities of life threw at us, the stronger it got. We became less optimistic and more doubtful, less assured and more uncertain, less confident and more unsettled. Have you ever taken the time to ask yourself why that is?

Your curiosity is trapped and being held hostage by the trauma of your experiences.

It's not that curiosity and courage don't exist deep inside you. It's just that they've been locked away in a dungeon for decades, 100,000 feet beneath the surface of the person you've become, and not the person you were born to be. They've been withering away, barely surviving and starving from thirst and hunger. They only get fed the occasional meal of hope and desire to keep them alive long enough so that you can go on existing. But what is life without curiosity? What is life without an eager wish to learn something new? The answer to that is quite simply, existence. That isn't life at all. You're in a constant state of stagnation.

But it is time for you to set them free. The only way to do that is to visit the dungeon. You must take the treacherous journey 100,000 feet underground, key in hand while shaking uncontrollably, to the place that you only visit every couple of years. This is the place you actually try to avoid at all costs, the place that you've made yourself forget about. Until now, you've been able to get by, and to everyone else, you have it all together. You seem to always have the right answers. People come to you to confide in you, to seek your counsel, and get your advice. They admire who you show them you are. Yes, they admire the performer...

...But if they only knew about your dungeon...

...Would they still admire you then?

If they knew you were afraid, would they come clamoring for your consultation? If they knew that you had locked away who you truly wish you could become, would they adore you as much?

This journey won't be an easy one because before you can even get to where you've held your destiny hostage, you have to go through the detour of trauma that's been caused by your life's experiences. You have to REMEMBER.

As you make this journey down into the deepest parts of your heart, the things you may see could be triggering. They may cause you pain, pain that you've avoided for a long time. That's the tricky thing about unlocking curiosity and courage, because in order for you to get to their holding cells, you have to pass everything you've been through that made you lock them away in the first place.

I want to tell you that everything that you've gone through has caused you to respond one of the two ways: lock it away, or let it go free.

I want to tell you that everything that you've gone through has caused you to respond one of the two ways: lock it away, or let it go free. I've locked things away. If we're honest, we've all locked some things away because they're just too agonizing to deal with. Rather than let them go, for some reason you'd rather hold on to the resentment because it gives you some sense of comfort. In order to deal with our traumas, it often means that we have to look at ourselves in the mirror. We have to either accept that what happened to us wasn't our fault, or we have to accept the role we played in our own demise. Whichever it is, it can be heart-wrenching to deal with either way.

For example, I remember long ago my brothers and I were outside just trying to find ways to make use of our boring lives. As a pre-teen, everything is boring to you if you're not being entertained in some way. I know this because my son is often bored and he sometimes makes it seem as if it is my job to keep him entertained. Anyhow, you know how you were when you were kids. You just created games to play. You tried to find things to do with your time. That's what we were doing. We came up with this neat game that involved roller skates and bikes. If you hadn't learned anything about my older brother and I, obviously, we had a taste for adventure.

The point of this game was for the person pedaling to pedal as fast as they could while the person on roller skates held onto the seat of the bike as long as they could. As I think about it, maybe it wasn't my brother who had the thrill for adventure; maybe it was me because I was always doing the most dangerous stuff. Of course, I volunteered to be the person on the roller blades. So, let the games begin!

I honestly think my brother had something to prove that day. He challenged me by saying,"Josh, you won't be able to hold on." Of course I responded, "Yes I will." After this, you know what comes next, right? We'd make a bet: whoever lost had to buy the winner whatever they wanted from the ice cream truck. Game on!

My brother started pedaling and I was holding on. It seemed quite easy at first but then he started to go faster, and faster, AND FASTER. As he picked up speed, my hands began slipping. I could feel myself losing my grip, but he still went faster. The wind started blowing in my face and it became harder for me to scream, "SLOW DOWN!" Even though I'm sure he heard my urgent cry for help, for some reason he picked up speed. He must have really wanted whatever it was from that ice cream truck. I felt my grip slipping continuously so I screamed, and screamed, AND SCREAMED, "SLOW DOWWNNNN!" Until finally, my hands slipped off of the seat of the bike. We were going so fast that there was no way I could maintain control. I spun out of control and slammed against the concrete. I skinned my face and my side.

You want to know what my response was to that excruciating experience? "I'll never do that again!" Isn't that our typical response to pain? We try to shield ourselves from it. We think that by avoiding it it's making us better, wiser. But that experience stole something from me that day. It stole a piece of my love for adventure. I needed to be more "careful", which means that I would inevitably take less risks in life.

A piece of who God created me to be was now in handcuffs.

A piece of who God created me to be was now in hand-cuffs. Instead of responding,"Hey, let's do it again when I heal up, but let's not go as fast this time around." That would have been a viable, wise option as well. Thing is, I didn't trust my brother. How could someone as close as family choose to inflict pain on someone he should love? I said, "I'll never do that again, ever!" Though it seemed like the sensible thing to do at that time because of the pain it caused in my present, I didn't realize the consequences that would reverberate into my future, ultimately changing me over time. If I can't trust my brother, then who can I trust?

I remember another time my father told me that I should always be a gentleman when it comes to how I treat women. Of course, my father was my hero, so if he says this, it is some-thing that I would take to heart. I wanted to be the man that my father said I should be because I wanted his acceptance and approval. I wanted to be a good man, and to make sure that the girl that I would choose as my girlfriend would know that I was a good man. I'd treat you right; never betray you, never cheat on you, win your trust, fight for your honor, and treat you with tender love and care.

I remember in the 8th grade I had taken a liking to this girl who will remain nameless. I had a crush on her. Finally I built up the courage to ask her,"Would you be my girlfriend? Circle: Yes, No, or Maybe So." To my surprise and excitement, she circled, "Yes." Cell phones weren't a thing at that time, so the only time we could talk was at school. We dated for a few weeks and those were the best weeks of my life. The euphoria quickly started to dwindle when I started to hear rumors that she started dating someone else. There's no way she would do this to me. What did I do? How could this be? I don't believe it.

Then, one morning while I was sitting at the table in the cafeteria with a few of my friends, my greatest fear had become a reality. She moved on. She walked into the school holding hands with another man, and at this time we were still dating. My head dropped. My countenance had fallen and I was embarrassed. "How could she do this to me?" is what I asked myself. I thought my dad said that I should always be a good man? But what has being a good man gotten me thus far? Brokenhearted, sad, and ashamed. Everyone was talking about me.

This was in 8th grade. Of course, I didn't know what I know now, and I wasn't able to contextualize this experience without making the assumption that girls don't want a good man. All I saw was her holding hands with the guy who was the opposite of me. He was the popular, charismatic trouble-maker that everyone loved. If girls wanted the good guy, then why would she choose him over me? The seed was planted, and all it took was a few more bad experiences with dating to make me come to the conclusion that if I wanted the girls of my dreams, I would have to become someone else.

In 10th grade, I dated someone that I had truly fallen for. We went to different schools, but that was ok because I trusted her, or so I thought. Though I hadn't yet given into the idea that girls don't want a good guy, the seed was planted. My experience in 8th grade just wouldn't allow me to walk around with my head in the clouds. No, I had to protect myself from any oncoming hurt. I wouldn't allow myself to be so free that I would be completely caught off guard again. But, she was beautiful. I couldn't help myself. I let my guards down. She used to run track and was a phenomenal athlete. Though I trusted her, the only problem that I had with her running track was that her ex-boyfriend went to the same school as her and ran track as well.

She had given me her word that she was over him and would never cross that line again, but one day we were on the phone and I could sense the change in her tone. She had a track meet earlier that day and you could feel the awkwardness in our conversation. I asked her, "What's wrong?" She responded, "Nothing. Eventually, I began to pry and she couldn't handle it anymore. She blurted out, "I KISSED HIM! I KISSED MY EX!"

I wasn't caught off guard as much as I was furious. I let you in! I didn't cheat on you! I didn't talk to other women! We had great conversations on the phone. But you kissed your ex! I will admit, the words that I used to describe her in that moment were not pleasant. I had been bamboozled again. These are just a few of the experiences I've had with dating, and I don't want to bore you with every story.

My dad's words rang in my ear, "Always be a gentleman, always be a good man." I remember her telling me how her ex talked to her, how he treated her, and how he cheated on her time and time again. It was bad, but because she "loved" him she gave him chance after chance. I just didn't understand how someone could treat you with such insolence and yet you go scurrying back to him. You betrayed the man who was the opposite of your ex. I actually loved you, or so I thought as a teenager in high school lol, and I showed you that through my actions.

After that experience, my 15-year old self came to a conclusion: my dad didn't have a clue. He didn't know what he was talking about. Sure, maybe in his day this is what girls wanted, but times have changed now. Girls don't want the good guy, they want the bad guy. Oh my, if you only knew how this simple change of mindset at 15 affected my relationships with women for years after.

You see, I was born to be a lover, someone who cared for people, and would go the extra mile to make sure people were taken care of, even if it was at the expense of my own sanity. I was thoughtful, considerate, easy going, trusting, jubilant, optimistic, trusting, lighthearted, idealistic, trusting, oh, did I forget to say trusting? Though my trust hadn't been completely ruined by her betrayal, the seed of distrust had been planted and watered enough to take root. Over time, those roots grew deeper and deeper.

But I want to explain a simple concept, and that concept is, it doesn't take big life-altering moments to change you.

I use these not-so-extreme examples, not because I don't have any other massive, life-altering examples to use. But I want to explain a simple concept, and that concept is, it doesn't take big life-altering moments to change you. Yes, big moments in your life can change you for sure. But do you want to know what has the most impact on your life that is frequently overlooked? It's the little moments, the little changes that go unnoticed but they change you over time.

Why? Because they're so small that they're easily overlooked. If you're honest, and you dig deep enough, you'll come to the conclusion that things you've labeled as "small" affected you deeply. It changed you. It put a part of you in handcuffs and sentenced that part of you to life in the dungeon. You probably figured that this is the best way to protect yourself from ever having to feel that emotion again.

But now it's time to set that part of you free so that you can get a piece of yourself back that you lost a long time ago. I'm a naturally trusting person, but because I had so many bad experiences with women, I began not to trust women...All women. But that isn't fair, is it? Why would I put all women in the same category when the reality is that I haven't dated all women? Also, why is it fair that I put all women in the same category when both of the women who betrayed me were only teenagers at the time? Is it fair to hold the sins of my teenage ex over my current partner's head even though she's never done anything to violate my trust? Is it ok that I subconsciously make my partner prove that she's trustworthy because I have trust issues? No, it's not ok.

Whether you know it or not, or whether you believe it or not, your experiences throughout life have chipped away at who you were born to be. You used to be outgoing, but then one day you arrived at a social gathering being your normal charismatic self, and someone sneered and told you that you were "doing too much", so you turned into an introvert. You used to be happy and hopeful, but then someone who you loved tragically lost their life to a drunk driver who got off with a slap on the risk.

You used to give freely but then someone took advantage of your generosity, so now you give skeptically hoping that your kindness isn't taken advantage of. You see what I mean? These experiences have caused you to change who you are. Whether it was because you didn't know how to deal with the trauma of what happened, or because you just wanted to be accepted, you changed and put your natural self in chains.

So how do you get that person back? How do you free yourself from the chains that you've placed yourself in? Well

I'll tell you this, it isn't easy because there's a lot of emotional work that needs to be done. Depending on how old you are, things become instinctual over time. They only become embedded more deeply into your personality and belief system. Reactions that weren't the norm before become patterns of behavior now. To address these behaviors, you'll need spiritual and professional help. For me, I identify as a Christian, so my relationship with God was a quintessential factor in helping change behaviors that I knew I had no ability to change on my own.

I also sought professional help as well. Whether by hiring a therapist or through reading books, you have to be relentless about removing yourself from those chains because they won't come off easily. As painful as the experiences were that put you in them, is as painful as it might be to remove them and set yourself free.

But one thing you cannot afford to do is let the trauma of your past keep you from the freedom you could experience in your present. When you're in bondage, you can never become who you were truly meant to be. You'll only see glimpses of the person you could possibly become. But if you want true freedom, and if you want to accomplish true purpose and destiny for your life, then it's time for you to dig deep, do the painful work of addressing your past, and finally free yourself from your dungeon.

I want you to start by asking yourself, what happened to that person I used to be? What changed me? When you're able to answer this, then you're able to truly start your journey to true freedom. Freedom to do what, you ask? Freedom to be you.

IT'S TIME TO LET THE SHAME GO

The hardest thing about facing and embracing our experiences is facing the shame that comes along with them. Most of the time when we experience something that makes us feel ashamed or embarrassed, we retreat or withdraw. Why? Because no one likes to feel humiliated. And people, especially men, don't want to feel weak and vulnerable. So as human beings, we tend to hide from the experience by trying to forget it happened, instead of embracing that the particular experience was a necessary part of our journey.

I know what you're thinking. If you've been through something deeply traumatizing like abuse, how could that be a necessary part of your journey? Could you not have become the person you are today without that experience? Possibly, but we can't say that with certainty because unfortunately, that's

ve asked yourself, why is this some-
hrough? My next question would be,
w if you had not gone through it and
.eans saying that you had to go through
. strong". I'm sure you could have been
the traumatization of such an experience.
ing is that if you allow it, the trauma of that
. make you wiser and stronger.

*you allow it, the trauma of that
ce could make you wiser and stronger.*

.nt you to think about it like this...what if that experi-
didn't happen "to you"? What if it happened "for you"?
.t I mean by that is simply a shift in mindset. When it
.ppens "to you", it's completely out of your control. You are
.ie victim and if you're not careful this experience will have
complete control over how you see and engage life in the
past, present, and future. When it happens "for you", even
though you couldn't stop it happening "to you", you make a
self-empowering decision to choose how you will respond to
that experience moving forward, and how you will allow that
experience to dictate your life.

Things happening "to you" render you powerless. Things
happening "for you" make you powerful. Why? Because the
latter lets your experiences empower you, you don't become a
slave to them.

When you hear someone always complain about how their experience has completely ruined their life, this is a person who has subconsciously accepted that they have no power to free themselves. They're held captive by the shame, embarrassment, or attention attached to the experience. Therefore, even if the experience was 10 years ago, they can't help but carry themselves like the victim, instead of the victor.

Can I tell you about one of my experiences? It's actually really embarrassing, so I hesitate to write about it even now. I was a part of the football team in the ninth grade. Now you may think that I was a popular kid in high school because of the platform that I've built on social media today. But I assure you that isn't the case. I wasn't a popular kid. I was regular. Yep, that's right, regular regular. I didn't hang with the cool kids, and I wasn't invited to the popular kid house parties. For the most part, I hung around a group of friends that lived in my neighborhood and we stayed to ourselves. I had to make sure I painted the picture so you know that I wasn't one of those kids. Despite how outgoing I am now, that wasn't the case in high school.

I remember one day after football practice I was sitting on the bench in the locker room taking off my shoulder pads and drinking some water. The other players were laughing and horse playing, while I was just minding my business. It was hot, I was tired, and ready to go home. While minding my business, one of the popular football players drafted me into this game that I didn't sign up for. What was the game? He slapped me...HARD...out of nowhere.

Where I come from, one of the most disrespectful things you can do to a person is slap them. Call me out my name. Punch me. But by no means should you slap me because that's saying I'm so weak that you don't even have enough respect for me to just punch me, so they just slap you instead. I would put slapping and spitting on someone in similar categories. The entire locker room was dying laughing after it happened. It was some sort of game to them. I was so shocked by the experience that I honestly didn't know what to do. Not only that, I was small and skinny at the time. So if I'm honest, I was scared too. I didn't have any friends on the football team, especially no one that would come to my defense and help me fight if that's what it came down to. I could have gotten jumped, stomped, or even worse. There was no coach in sight to stop it if we started fighting. So you know what I did? I sat there. Almost in tears from embarrassment and anger, I just sat there and let them laugh at me. It was probably one of the most embarrassing moments of my life.

True enough, I was the victim in that situation. What happened to me, I didn't deserve. But I had a choice to make now because I couldn't change what he did. Yet, I could choose the person I become from that moment on. I could shrink in fear; walk around timidly; quit the football team; avoid him at all costs in the hallway; hang my head low when I ran across any of the football players that witnessed what he did. I could feel sorry for myself. and could have justified my reasoning for not playing sports anymore because all athletes were jerks. I could have developed an unwarranted disdain for jocks, but I didn't. You want to know why? Because even though I can't change what happened, I could control how I responded to it. I let that situation empower me, not enslave me.

...even though I can't change what happened, I could control how I responded to it. I let that situation empower me, not enslave me.

So who did I become? I don't know if it is the greatest outcome, but I promised myself that I would not let that ever happen to me again. I didn't allow myself to live from a place of victimization. So, I became a fighter. I learned how to defend myself and force myself to look fear and intimidation in the eyes and say, "No, no matter who you are, how big you are, or how muscular you are, I will never be afraid of anyone again." I didn't allow that experience to trap me in shame and embarrassment.

Here's the thing about shame. That emotion makes you want to hide and isolate yourself. Does that remind you of something that we talked about in the previous chapter? That's right, the dungeon. Shame will make you lock yourself away in a dungeon. It makes you want to succumb and be overthrown by the negative opinions that you have of yourself. There's no way that you can boldly step into the light and accept who you were born to be because shame is the antithesis of bravery. How can you be brave if you're overcome with shame? It's an unpleasant, self-conscious emotion often associated with negative self-evaluation; motivation to quit; and feelings of pain, exposure, distrust, powerlessness, and worthlessness.

Maybe you think that the things you've gone through are your fault, or you feel like if you did something differently it would not have happened the way it did. Maybe you're right, maybe that's the case. Thing is, you can't change the past, but you can change the present. I want you to accept and see the beauty in your experiences no matter how ugly they are to look at. Accept that you aren't perfect. Accept that you've made mistakes. Accept that whatever has happened to you, from the neighborhood you were raised in, to the job you were unfairly fired from, happened to inevitably mold you into the person you are today.

Now you can choose to be the person that life happens to. You can choose to go throughout life and feel like you have limited control of its direction. But choosing that route will render you helpless, always waiting for the right situation or person to save you. You'll always feel like your back is against the ropes as negative situations in your life continue to pile on. You'll always be on the defensive. There's a saying in sports that defense wins games, but that's a lie.

The point of competitive sports is to have more points than the other team at the end of the game. If you only played defense there's no way you would ever score. A better saying would probably be that defense puts you in a better position to strike back. To make your move. Like a lion who quietly waits to pounce on its prey, you wait for the right moment to go for it and take advantage of your opponent's mistakes. There's a purpose and a reason for everything you've been through. Once you accept that, you grant yourself permission to use your experience as fuel to propel you to the next level.

IDENTIFYING YOUR GIFTS

Have you ever received a present on a day like Christmas or your birthday? I must admit getting gifts is one of the best things about birthdays. You feel seen. You feel appreciated. You feel like you haven't been forgotten about. I can remember a time when I was a child I gave one of my brothers a gift for his birthday. It was one of my favorite Dragon Ball Z action figures. Since I wasn't old enough to work and I didn't have any money, this was the best that I could do. But it's the thought that counts, right?

I remember the hesitancy I had just before I was about to give him the gift. I had expectations and didn't even know it. "He'd better play with Goku like I do," I said to myself. "This better not be a waste." "Do I really want to give him this, what if he breaks it?" All of these thoughts I had going on in my head as a kid because I didn't want to give up my favorite toy.

But I wanted to do something nice for my brother, and I'm sure he knew how important it was to me that I was giving him my favorite action figure. Never-the-less on his birthday, encouraged by my mom, I said, "Happy Birthday" to my brother and gifted him with my toy. My mom said, "Now what are you supposed to say, Leon?"

He looked at her confused because he honestly didn't know what to say, and then she said, "Say thank you." So he said, "Thank you." and she said, "Now go and give your brother a hug." Everyone standing around watching was like, "Awwww, that's so cuttteeee!" And then what happened next invigorated me. He dropped my action figure on the floor and moved on to the next toy that he really wanted to play with. I couldn't blame him though because the Power Wheels were definitely out of my league, but I still felt some type of way about him dropping my gift on the ground, never to be played with again.

I would take my revenge. How, you ask? I took my action figure back. He never knew because he never cared for it. He never played with the darn thing anyway. So one day, weeks later, he finally wanted to play with the action figure and we fought over it. He was crying and claiming that the toy was "mine". I screamed, "No it's not, it's mine!" My mom rushed into the room and asked us, "What's going on here?" I told her that he's trying to play with "my" toy. She asked, "Didn't you give this to him on his birthday?" I said, "Yes, but he never played with it so I took it back!" Her response was, "That's wrong Joshua, you shouldn't give gifts and then take them back, that means you really didn't want him to have the

action figure in the first place. That's being an Indian giver."
You know what, she was right. I really never wanted to give
him "my" action figure. If it was truly a gift, then it was no
longer "my" action figure, it was "his" action figure now.

The reason I'm telling you this story is because usually when
someone gives you a gift, they shouldn't expect anything in
return. Or at least that's how it should be anyway. They're not
giving you the gift to hear you say thank you; to see your face
light up with excitement; to see if you're ever going to use it,
or if it's going to be buried in a drawer somewhere.

They gave you the gift because they thought enough about
you that they wanted you to have it. Now some people give
sucky gifts with no thought or intentionality behind it. They
didn't take the time to pay attention to who you are. They
didn't listen to you when you spoke about how you always
wanted to travel to a certain place. They actually forgot it was
a special day and so they made a last ditch effort to get you
something so that they wouldn't feel bad for forgetting. I'm not
talking about those types of people when it comes to giving
gifts. Even still, they didn't have to get you anything at all.

But I'm referring to the kind of giver who has taken time
to know your likes and dislikes. When they give you a gift, it's
usually something thoughtful and they don't expect anything
in return for it. I want you to know something, the day you
were born you were given gifts. You were given the gift of life,
and the gifts of your God-given talents.

I want to use this chapter to help you identify your gifts so that you can go out into the world and influence others through the things that you are naturally gifted at. That's what a gift is. A gift is something that you don't have to try hard at. It's something that comes naturally to you. If you have to "try hard" at it then it's probably not a gift.

When you were born, you were wonderfully and uniquely created. This means that there is no other person in the world like you. There's no one who could duplicate you. There's no one who could do what you do the way you do it. Even if you were born as an identical twin, you're still exclusively distinctive. You have your nuances that make you different, special, and unique. Along with your gift of life came the gift of your talents. Things that you didn't have to hammer away at to be good at. You've probably seen people struggle with the very things that came effortlessly to you. These are your gifts and you have them because they're a part of your greater purpose.

Everyone has gifts. These talents were freely given to us so that we could make a unique impact on the world. Think about it. What if we were all the same? I just literally threw up in my mouth at the thought. What if there was nothing different about everyone in the world? Do you think we would be further ahead or further behind if this were the case? I would say the latter. What if there were a bunch of "you's" walking around? Can you imagine how uninspiring life would be, how we would not have the technological advances that we have now if we were a carbon-copy of each other? You know how many things wouldn't exist if we were exactly alike? Because that would mean we'd all have the same thoughts, approach, and reactions. There would be no space for ingenuity and innovation. Thank God that is not the case. No, we are different, purposefully so.

I want to definitively make my next statement:The most tragic thing you could do with your life is to waste your gifts.

Do you know that most people don't ever live up to their true potential? They spend most of their time trying to do what other people are gifted at instead of tapping into their own gifts. But that's another story for another chapter. They'll never reach their greatest potential because they're not doing what they enjoy. When you're doing what you enjoy, it never feels like work because you get true fulfillment out of it. This alone will keep you inspired and motivated. Even when you experience failures, you'll keep going because you couldn't stop if you wanted to. Why? You're just too darn good at it. It's your gift.

When you're not doing the things that bring you real gratification, you have to practically make yourself show up. It becomes forced. It becomes ROUTINE. Routine, most times, is the enemy of progress. Routine helps you stay disciplined, but it flees from anything that looks unfamiliar because the unfamiliar puts you in conflict with your routine, and unfamiliar means change. People hate change. But oftentimes, to access the true extent of your gifts, change is imminent. Though change can be difficult because it's different, if you trust your instinct and start aligning your life with your gifts, you'll begin living a life that's filled with happiness and meaning. So the question is, how do you identify your gifts? I'm glad you asked.

I partly gave you the answer to that question earlier. Your gifts are things you are naturally good at, so ask yourself, what comes easy or naturally to you? I'll use myself as an example. One of the things that I'm naturally good at is creativity. I'm naturally creative so creativity is my gift. That's one of the reasons why I'm able to write books, scripts, and even music so quickly. It's because I have a very creative lucid imagination. Did you know that something like creativity could be a gift? Through creativity, I can often visualize things before they manifest into real form. I can see it before I see it, or, I can see it and then will it into existence. Because I'm so creative, it translates into skills that I've acquired over the years.

There's a difference between your gifts and skills. Your gift shines through your skills. Gifts are instinctive, but skills are something you have to work at to become proficient in. Lebron James is a naturally gifted athlete. What I mean is that he was born with the physique of someone who could play sports, but that doesn't mean that he would naturally be good at basketball. Sure, he'd have an advantage at any sport he chose to dedicate himself to because of his size but he would still need to develop his skills for any sport he chose, and that sport was basketball. He had to work hard and develop his skills to become a great basketball player. Lebron was naturally born with a high IQ. This is why he's able to assess situations and make the right decisions quickly on the court. If you're familiar with basketball, then you know that they often say he has "court vision". His vision is his gift. Him being able to execute that vision at a high level is his skill.

I may be able to imagine how a really dope design should look for an event flier, but that doesn't mean that I understand how to use and operate Adobe Photoshop. I would need to acquire the skills to be able to operate Adobe Photoshop proficiently. I may have the creative vision to see exactly how I want my new website to look, but that doesn't mean that I have the skills to actually go and build the website myself. Those are skills that I would need to go and acquire.

Let me explain. Through my creativity I've picked up a few skills overtime like:

- Graphic Design
- Website Design
- & Marketing

My gift of creativity allows me to be able to visualize what things should look like before they're ever manifested. BUT, now I have to go acquire the skills to make my vision a reality. So for me, I had to go and learn how to use photoshop to create business cards and fliers for myself and other businesses. As an artist, if I wanted to be taken seriously, I needed a website. Well, I knew how the website should look but I didn't know how to build one, so I had to learn how to build websites on platforms like Wordpress. I also knew that if I wanted to be taken seriously as an artist, I needed a music video. I envisioned exactly how I wanted the video to look but I didn't have the budget to pay someone to shoot it for me.

So, I learned how to edit videos using Adobe Premiere myself. That's a skill I learned over time. Though I may be good at putting words on paper, it doesn't mean that I knew how to write in such a way that would convince people to buy something I was selling. No, I had to learn how to write sales copy. That's a skill that I acquired through my gift. Now that I learned how to write sales copy, I needed to be able to understand how to get that copy in front of people who were eager to buy whatever it was that I was selling, so I educated myself on Facebook ads.

You see what I mean here? I honed my gift and then learned the skills necessary to really make them shine and come to life.

Let me give you another example of my gifts. I have the gift of charisma and influence. I can literally influence just about anyone to buy into my vision. I can walk into a room, not trying to get attention but for some reason, people are interested in what I have to say. But just because I have the gift of influence and charisma it doesn't mean that I have the skills to be a great leader. Those are skills that I would need to develop overtime through intentionality, application, and experience. Just because I'm charismatic, it doesn't mean that I'm patient. Just because I'm charismatic doesn't mean that I know how to show empathy or how to be a strategic, critical thinker. These are skills that I need to acquire to bolster my natural gift of influence so that I can become the leader I was meant to be.

The problem with most people is that they go and acquire skills that have nothing to do with their gifts. For example, you become an engineer because you don't want to be a failure in the eyes of your parents, but in your spare time, you like to paint. Well, painting has nothing to do with engineering. Painting is art. Engineering is science. But you spend the majority of your time engineering because you don't want to be looked at as a failure and disappointment. So now, you have a skill that you don't love that is consuming most of your time when it should be the other way around. Your time is being spent on acquiring skills that don't bolster your gifts. Your gifts should be influencing your skills.

You should be spending time changing the world through the things you naturally enjoy and are exceptional at.

You should be spending time changing the world through the things you naturally enjoy and are exceptional at. You torment yourself trying to buckle down and pass that engineering exam when you should really be preparing to host your first art show. Sure, you can learn soft skills through anything you apply yourself to, but the point is to prioritize your gifts and then learn the skills you need to dominate and make them shine. This is where you'll be the happiest.

The world has taught us to prioritize money over our purpose, so we spend time trying to lay the foundation financially by investing an enormous amount of our time into things that will make us financially secure. The caveat here is all of that time we've spent investing into skills that don't align with our gifts is time that we can never get back. But money should never be the priority. Passion, love, and serving people through your gifts should be the priority. If you truly understand how powerful this is, then you know that the money would come if you did this, if you prioritized people over profits.

Your priority shouldn't be making money. Your priority should be focused on honing your gifts. If you hone your gifts, you will find ways to monetize them. But just because your gifts come natural to you, it doesn't mean that you won't have to do any work to get the skills you need to hone them. I think some people may have misread my statement earlier. Yes, your gifts come EASY to you, but tapping into your greatness and manifesting the life you want to build for yourself will be far from EASY. And guess what? It's going to take time.

Here are a few quality examples that can be gifts to help point you in the right direction:

Examples Of Potential Gifts

Gift	Defined As:
Creativity	This person usually has the gift to generate ideas, solutions or insights that are strikingly original, and yet feasible:
Influence	The capacity to have an effect on the character, development, or behavior of someone or something, or the effect itself.
Empathy	Someone who feels more empathy than the average person. These people are usually more accurate in recognizing and feeling another's emotions.
Speaking/Communication	Conveying ideas effectively and identifying messages others are attempting to convey.
Music	This person can do everything you'd expect a highly-talented musician to do with practice, listening, and effort, naturally.

Administration	This person thrives when called upon to organize people to accomplish an objective.
Visionary	Visionaries see what's possible and make it happen. They are outspoken, self confident, and competitive.
Strategy	Strategic people understand the importance of being decisive in their decision-making.They recognize that reaching conclusions and being decisive takes both knowledge and confidence.
Wisdom/Decision Making	This person has a gift to make wise high-quality decisions based on limited information.
Conflict Resolution	This person has a gift of bringing others together to resolve conflict and reconcile differences.
Innovation	This person has a gift to generate solutions and creative ideas to solve problems.

Execution	This person has a natural knack to set goals, monitor progress, and take the initiative to improve their work.

Of course, there are plenty more gifts that I didn't identify here, but the point is to get your wheels turning.

Another way to recognize some of your strongest gifts is to pay attention to what other people say about you. Has your boss ever come to you and thanked you for something specific that you did? Maybe that could have been going the extra mile to make sure the event went off without a hitch. Maybe you managed a team who lacked direction and enthusiasm, or made sure that the communication went out on time everytime, so that everyone knew exactly what they were supposed to be doing when they were supposed to be doing it.

Have your friends ever come to you and said, "You're so good at that!"? What's the thing that they said you were so good at? Could it be that when they needed to organize their birthday party, they came to ask for your help? Could it be that you have a strong network and a lot of people like you so they'd like you to be in charge of corralling the people?

What about your parents? I bet if you asked your parents what they have come to learn about you since knowing you, they could give you some insight. I mean, they have been in your life since you were born...hopefully...*cringing*. Maybe they noticed something special about you as a child that you forgot about, or never really took the time to investigate. You probably thought to yourself, "I'm sure all kids are like this...", but they aren't. You're just naturally gifted in that area; you didn't have to earn it or try hard.

If you have to "earn" your gift, then it's not a gift. Things that you "earn" are skills you develop overtime. There's a difference between earning and honing your gift. Think about it like this...you go to work because you have to earn your wage. But if you decided to stop working, then that means you wouldn't get paid. Earning is defined as receiving as return for effort, especially for work done or services rendered. A gift can be defined as something voluntarily transferred by one person to another without compensation.

That's the difference between earning a skill and tapping into your gifting. Earning a skill means that if you ever stopped, if you ever decided not to show up, that skill would diminish, and you wouldn't reap the rewards. But with your gift, no matter if you decided to show up or not, you would still be exceptional at it without even really trying. This means that you would still be able to benefit from it whether you were trying to or not. You would still be good at this thing that you were given when you were born. It was freely given to you. You just have to hone it; refine or perfect it over time.

People often have trouble identifying what their gifts are when the answer is staring them in the face. In most cases, they just can't see it because they aren't taught to look for it, or they can't see it because it comes so naturally to them that they just overlook it. But you are gifted, and the sooner you start living from a place that prioritizes your gifts, you'll start walking in your purpose like never before.

CHAPTER

5

OVERCOMING YOUR COMFORT

"THE ENEMY OF PROGRESS IS ROUTINE, AND ROU-
TINE IS NURTURED IN COMFORT."

The enemy of progress is routine, and routine is nurtured in comfort. Routine can be a good thing if it doesn't handicap you from coloring outside the lines and trying something new. But if it does, your routine is more of a hindrance than a help. To help you get out of your comfort zone, you must break your routine. The reason routines are so hard to break is because there's no fear in routine. Fear only comes from the place of the unknown.

Routine can be a good thing if it doesn't
handicap you from coloring outside the lines
and trying something new. But if it does, your
routine is more of a hindrance than a help.

Your routine is known. It is predictable. You know that if you stick to your routine, things will go according to plan. Plans are certain, especially when you've developed a methodical way of doing things. Wake up. Brush your teeth. Wash your face. Get ready for work. Put on your favorite fragrance. Clock in. Greet your colleagues. Man your station. Check your emails. Attend your meetings. Take lunch. Work on your project. Mentally tap out as time gets closer for you to clock out. Clock out. Go home. Pick up dinner. Have a drink. Read a book. Scroll social media. Watch your favorite show. Take a shower. Jump in bed. Set your alarm clock. Go to sleep. Alarm goes off. Hit the snooze button. Wake up and do it all over again. You see, even within your normal, every-day life, you have a routine, a plan.

Plans grant you permission to create routines that avoid discomfort at all costs.

Plans grant you permission to create routines that avoid discomfort at all costs. Plans are never full proof. Actually, rarely do things ever go "according to plan". That's unless you program your life so meticulously that it doesn't leave room for growth, excitement, and the unexpected. People rarely like deviating from the plan because the plan gives you a false sense of reality. You've created a life that you can control, only to realize that you're really not in control at all. With a stroke of a pen, a pandemic can hit and completely end life as you once knew it. Plans provide the illusion that everything is going to be ok as long as you follow the plan. But once you break free from your plan, or your need to be in control, now fear enters the equation. And fear is rarely ever a part of the plan, because fear makes you uncomfortable.

Have you ever watched a suspenseful movie where someone frantically searches a home for answers? Let me set the stage for you. Johnny always knew that his step dad, "Robert", was hiding something. He could never prove it but he knew that, though Robert presented himself as a righteous man, something about him just didn't sit right with Johnny. Johnny oftentimes ignored his gut and convinced himself that he had no reason not to trust Robert. Robert was faithful to his mom. Robert went to work every day and came home at the same time. Robert even bought this new house that they moved into. Johnny likes the neighborhood, has started making friends, and his mom seems to be the happiest he's ever seen her. But why does something still feel..."off"? Maybe this feeling Johnny felt is just because Robert and Johnny's mom have only been married 2 years, and it's still taking some time to get used to Robert. Maybe this feeling is nothing. Nevertheless, Johnny can't shake the feeling.

One day Johnny couldn't sleep, so he went downstairs to get him some water from the kitchen, hoping to cool his hot body down. It seemed like the air was broken. To his surprise, he hears a slight sound coming from a tv in the living room. Who would be up at this hour? Afraid, Johnny slowly makes his way down stairs. Then, he hears the door to the garage open...it was Robert. He was sweating, out of breath, and nervous. Johnny had never seen Robert like this before. Johnny slowly takes a few steps backwards and hides behind the corner. Robert turns off the tv and then retreats to the master bedroom to call it a night.

As Johnny silently waits, he's thinking to himself, "What would make Mr. Robert so uneasy?" "What's in the garage?" Fear grips Johnny. He knows that his apprehension of Mr. Robert has led him to this moment. The moment of truth. Johnny is committed to finding out what Mr. Robert has been hiding. So, Johnny quietly makes his way to the garage and as he gets closer, fear starts to set in. "What if he gets caught?" Johnny thinks to himself, "What if the thing that he finds changes him and his mom's life forever?" "Is it even worth it?" "What if I'm tripping?" Johnny's mind is being bombarded with questions. He's started to second guess and convince himself that maybe this is all in his head and Mr. Robert was probably outside just trying to fix the air conditioner. Then, Johnny convinces himself, "Yes, that must be the case, there isn't anything suspicious going on, it's all in my head." Satisfied with that resolve, Johnny aborts his mission and makes his way back up to the room and falls asleep.

Here are a few things that I want you to know about Johnny. As soon as Johnny had the opportunity to break the routine and find out the truth, fear set in. Fear convinced Johnny to turn around and go back to his room. Fear made Johnny go against his instinct and intuition. Johnny was being objective; yeah sure, Mr Robert could have just been outside trying to fix the a/c so that his family could sleep comfortably. Or, Mr. Robert could have been panicking because the freezer that was under lock and key had a woman's cold body in it. Mr. Robert knew that without electricity, the body would start to decay and smell. This would bring attention to his hideous hobby. Mr. Robert was secretly a serial killer. Extreme, I know, but follow me.

Johnny had gotten so accustomed to this new life that had been provided by Mr. Robert, he risked him and his mom's safety by going against his instinct. That's what routine will do to you. Johnny didn't want to lose that life.

How many times has your fear and instinct been in opposition with each other? How many times in the heat of battle has your fear prevailed over your instinct? That can be the danger of routine, it leaves no room for fear and allows you to continue life with this false sense of control. Johnny didn't want to lose that life. He didn't want to lose his friends. He didn't want him and his mom to have to start all over again. Things were going so well. Mom had just got a promotion. Johnny just made the basketball team and was becoming popular amongst his peers. It was all so perfect.

That is, until, a new detective starts sniffing around who had a close eye on Mr. Robert for months. Johnny didn't know about the detective and Mr. Detective was closing in fast. Soon enough, the life that Johnny and his mom had come to love was about to explode anyway.

This is usually how life works. You try to plan for every contingency to hold on to what you have. But then things begin to happen that are beyond your control; for instance, layoffs at the job because the executive staff misappropriated funds; the company gets bought out and during the transition they're bringing in a new team, so it's out with the old and in with the new; your spouse just tells you one day that they're not happy and they haven't been happy for a long time. They want a divorce; you finally get pregant only to have a miscarriage; the career you've worked so hard to build would be fulfilling, but now that you made it to the top, you feel empty, or you find out that you were adopted well into your adulthood and this news has completely reshaped your identity.

The point is, life will throw curve balls that you couldn't prepare for, even if you tried. And usually when these things happen, you start to sit back and really evaluate what's most important. Why am I here? Why am I unhappy? Why do I feel...desolate?

This is because comfort has forced you into a life void of excitement and significance. Oftentimes, the house has to be on fire for people to get out of it. But the thing is you smelt the gas leak long before the house ever caught on fire...you just got used to the smell. It was small, a hint of gas, not enough to be alarmed. And since you couldn't find the leak, you didn't bother with it. Soon enough, you couldn't smell the gas anymore. Has this ever happened to you? You walked into a place and you smelled something terrible, but after a few minutes it seems like the smell went away? That's the thing. The smell never went away, you just got used to the smell so you didn't smell it anymore. The problem is still there until you resolve it. But if you're not careful, you'll become so complacent that you will only give the problem more time to fester, grow, and get worse. Next thing you know, the gas leak has caught fire and you have no choice but to lose your home.

This is what comfort does to us. We know that there's a problem, but since we can't immediately identify what that problem is, we ignore it hoping that it goes away eventually. We hope that the problem course corrects and solves itself. Soon enough, we forget that the problem even exists. The problem grows. The resentment grows. And now it's so big that it can't be ignored. This is what comfort does to us. It allows us the illusion of relaxation in the very thing that's corroding us from the inside out.

Let me ask you, when was the last time you really challenged yourself, lived beyond your limits, stopped playing it safe and faced rejection and fear head on, or welcomed the thought of being terribly uncomfortable? If you're having a hard time identifying a time when you jumped into the deep end of your life knowing that you don't know how to swim, the harsh reality is that you've spent most of your life living in your comfort zone. You don't have to fear the pool because you've always stayed on the shallow end of it, the place that's safe. If anything ever went wrong, you know that you're in the safety of 3 feet of water. You're tall enough for your feet to touch the ground if you ever got into trouble. But if the water is deeper, you have no choice but to put your true swimming skills to the test because it's live or die.

How is it that the majority of human beings have allowed themselves to live most of their life in the comfort zone? Well, the answer to that question is simple: they've rationalized their way into the ordinary. Could you imagine that most people have rationalized their way out of their purpose? To be rational means to base your decision making on reason and logic. Does it sound reasonable to jeopardize the life you've built for the life you want? Of course it doesn't. If you spent most of your life pursuing a career that provided you with financial security, does it sound rational to give it up now to become a starving artist? No, that sounds completely crazy, right? Why would you give up a career that you've invested years into building that's given you a sense of stability to "chase your dreams"? To any sane person, that would sound insane because that isn't reasonable. You would quit your career as an engineer to become a "painter"? You must have lost it!

But honestly, most people will gladly sacrifice their happiness for a job that provides them with the lifestyle that they desire. They desire to live in condos and high rises. They desire to jet set and take trips. Is being a painter going to allow them to be able to live that lifestyle? It could. But to them, it's not likely. They've been told by their parents, family, and friends what career path they should take. And sure, they won't outright shoot down your dreams when you express them to the people you love.

But they'll say things like,

"I think that's great, BUT you should always have a plan B."

If they think what you want to do with your life is so great, then why would you ever need a plan B? Sure, you've been told to follow your dreams, but as soon as you tell them what your dreams are, you can sense the pessimism in their voice because your dreams are unconventional. Your dream doesn't fit inside the box of what normal success looks like. So because you care about what they think, you sacrifice a life filled with meaning and substance for a life of safety and stability.

But here's the thing. Stability only strips you from freedom. Stability will have you serving life in a jail called your comfort zone. And your comfort zone has now built you a life that you are now a slave to: a life in chains; chains to bills; chains to expenses; chains to exquisite dinners, and fancy vacations; chains to the expectations and opinions of others, and chains to the acceptance and affirmation of family and friends.

Most people postpone a perpetual life of happiness and fulfillment so that they can experience things in the short term that they think will make them happy in the long run. Sure, the vacation may feel good for a moment, but the truth is, you had to get permission to go on vacation. Someone had to tell you when you have permission to take time off. And the truth is, you don't spend most of your life on vacation, do you? You spend most of your time working a job that drains any motivation you have for more. When you do make it home from work, you don't have the mental space for anything else. See, you might be happy in the moment, but what I'm challenging you to think about is happiness for a lifetime, not waiting until you've lost the courage, energy, and motivation of your youth to finally retire, kick back and relax. There's no such thing as retirement for people who have dedicated their lives to their purpose. If you truly want to start living NOW, you'll need to start by breaking out of jail. Reject what makes you comfortable and start planning your escape.

You need to ask yourself what do you really want out of your life? And can you obtain whatever that is living in your comfort zone? I do understand the responsibilities that come with being an adult, and the pressure that comes with trying to live up to other people's expectations. Bills are real. And the things that you've accumulated overtime have helped you feel a sense of accomplishment. That's why it can be so difficult to let certain things go. But to walk in your purpose, you have to ask yourself what you are willing to sacrifice and how bad do you want it. How much of a priority is it for you to become who you were born to be?

I'm not saying that you should become an entrepreneur, because entrepreneurship isn't for everyone. But I am saying that for you to take your life by the horns, you will need to adapt an entrepreneurial mindset. Entrepreneurs don't wait for permission. They forge the way. Entrepreneurs don't seek the acceptance of people. They act on their instinct and accept the consequences of charting their own course with open arms. Being an entrepreneur means that you're in charge. Even if you don't want to become an entrepreneur by owning your own business, EVERYONE needs to be the founder and CEO of their own life. So, even if you don't want to start a business, you need to adapt an entrepreneurial mindset to walk in your purpose.

Being an entrepreneur is more about mindset than anything else...but I get it...

Entrepreneurship is probably the scariest thing you'll ever do because you rid yourself of every handicap when you adopt an entrepreneurial mindset. You can't depend on a weekly check. You release yourself from the comfort of knowing how you're going to pay the rent when the 1st comes around. If it fails, IT'S ON YOU. If it doesn't work, it's your fault. Being an entrepreneur just became popular in the last 5 years. But to be honest, most people don't really want to be an entrepreneur. They're just attracted to the lifestyle they see on social media; the yachts, the fancy cars, the high rises, the expensive dinners, and the laptop lifestyle. But that's the life that people show you because it's aspirational. People love to see what they cannot have. Who wouldn't want to live a life like that? The reality is, it's much more cold and lonely than what you see on your news feed.

When people used to ask what you did for a living and you responded, "I'm an entrepreneur", they would scoff under their breath and then follow up with a question like, "Yeah but...what do you do for a living, like, what's your day job?" You could tell that they didn't take you seriously. Now, being an entrepreneur is more appealing, but it's all for the wrong reasons. People want the lifestyle without the process and without mental fortitude. But you will never get the lifestyle without the process, and the process is very uncomfortable.

That's why the entrepreneurial mindset is essential for living a life of mission and purpose. Because you have to consciously choose a life of uncertainty over a life of pre-dictability, you have to accept that life won't get easier. It will only get harder. You have to accept failure and mistakes. You'll have to reject your inherent need for perfectionism and things going according to plan. The entrepreneurial mindset welcomes the confusion of discomfort.

Sure, you look at the glamorous lifestyle you see on social media and you think to yourself, that's what I want. But is it? That lifestyle is hard. And oftentimes, people avoid hard for what's common, not for what's easy. If people intrinsically wanted it easy, they would avoid all the effort it takes to get their degree or certification. They have to study and discipline themselves, and get a tutor for the subjects they have a hard time grasping.

Would a person put forth all of this effort if they wanted it to come easy? No. People don't want easy. **People want familiar**. They want to follow a proven record of success. The problem with following someone else's proven track record, is purely that. It's their track record, not your own. And just because it worked for them, it doesn't mean that it's going to work for you.

The reason why a plan is so appealing is because humans want to mitigate risks. What does that mean? Risk mitigation involves taking action to reduce one's exposure to potential risks, and reduce the likelihood that those risks will happen again. A risk can be defined as exposing (someone or *something of value*) to danger, harm, or loss. When you mitigate risks, your goal is to lessen the severity, seriousness, or pain that can be inflicted by the risk taken. Your aim is to avoid danger, harm, and loss at all cost. This is what people spend most of their life doing. They don't necessarily want the easy route. They just want to avoid as much pain and uncertainty as possible along the way. The best way to do this is to follow someone else's path in hopes that you experience the same level of success that they have. But because this path is not your own, you subsequently end up living a miserable life, a duplicate of someone else, trapped in their maze.

When you live your life trying to avoid as much harm, danger, risk, loss, and pain as possible, you'll never meet the person you have the potential to become.

When you live your life trying to avoid as much harm, danger, risk, loss, and pain as possible, you'll never meet the person you have the potential to become. For this person to be awakened in you, they must be put in situations that challenge them to break out of their comfort zone. Courage is found in fear. Strength is found in weakness. Faith is found in doubt. If you avoid fear at all costs, how will you ever find courage? Can you truly appreciate light without the uneasiness of darkness? How would you ever know that you have the ability to fight if you've never been in one? Because you're afraid of getting a black eye, you avoid fights at all cost. But most wounds heal. Scientifically speaking, when you're wounded, within 3 months, the wound is almost as strong in its repair as it was before the trauma. You will heal. You will make it through this. You will become stronger, that's the benefit to not spending your life evading danger.

There's beauty in trouble and difficulty. Of course, when you're in the middle of it, it's hard to see the beauty in it. But there's beauty in evolution. There's beauty in accepting that most likely things will become troublesome before they improve, and result in you tapping into your superior self. I imagine that you probably wouldn't evolve at all without trials and tribulations. Conflict often comes before harmony and alignment. Human beings have this unique ability to adapt and overcome. Many times, our progression is stunted without tasting adversity. This life is all about evolution and becoming your greater self. So how do you accomplish that if you never look calamity in the eyes and dare it to make a move?

You want to know one of the most important parts of a championship fight between two boxers? It's the first time they meet in the ring. The first time these two professional fighters come from their corners and stare each other in the eyes as the referee reads them the rules. Whoever looks away, looks down, and is afraid to look their opponent in the eyes has likely already lost the fight. Boxing is the most dangerous sport in the world. But it's more mental than anything else. If you've already lost in your mind, you will likely lose in the ring. A fighter can smell the stitch of fear from miles away. Even if you are nervous, you must not show it or your opponent will pick up and capitalize on it. Literally, you can be killed with one blow, one wrong move. You must not start the fight by giving your opponent the advantage from the beginning by letting them sense your fear.

The ring is the next stage of your life. It's your opportunity to ascend into greatness and become a champion, a chance for your name to echo through history as one of the best to ever do it. The only thing stopping you is the opponent across the ring looking to make sure you never reach your destiny. Your opponent is your comfort zone. It will not bow out. It will not surrender or admit defeat. If you want to overcome your comfort, you must do something that makes you extremely uncomfortable, makes you nervous, strikes fear in your heart, and challenges you to face it head on. What's that thing for you? Whatever that thing is, that's where your next level resides.

For some people, that may be leaving their career and forging a new path. For others, that may be putting 100% of their time and attention into their passion and purpose, or strategically taking steps to transition into their next season. But for everybody who seeks to break out of their comfort zone, they know that they must take immediate action. This can no longer be put off or delayed.

I want you to know something, it is only the future that excites us. The past or present could never stir up our desire like the future can. We as human beings have always had an appetite for what's next. The reason that excitement has seemed stagnant within you is because you have become too relaxed in your present. The view of your future has become cloudy. So with time, your relaxation has slowly robbed you of any anticipation of what could be next. The comfort of your present has hijacked the motivation of your future. This has only allowed resentment to fester. If you want your excitement back, I want you to do this one thing for me: Start dreaming again.

Start thinking about what it could be like to become the person you were born to be. What could life be like if you lived outside of your comfort zone? What could life be like for you if you didn't live within the confines of "could've" and "should've"? What could happen if you allowed your imagination to run wild? What would you imagine? As children, we don't know what it's like to live within limits because we spend most of our childhood being told that we can be anything we want to be. The most powerful thing about that is, as children, we believe it. Therefore, we don't think or imagine within the confines of the responsibilities and limits that we have as adults. Our imagination is free to run wild without limitation.

If our comfort zone has robbed us of anything, it would have to be the imagination of what our future could be if we just believed it enough to act on it. Imagination will do two things: it will agitate us in our present, while nudging us into our future. There's a difference between being content and comfortable. Contentment is a state of happiness and satisfaction regardless of the circumstances you face. Comfort is a state of physical ease and freedom from pain or constraint. You should always be content, but you should never become comfortable because comfortability is really just an illusion. There's no such thing as freedom from pain, resistance, or constraint. You may have freedom for a time, but it will only be for a time. Challenges are sure to come. It's just not a reality for people who are obsessed with tapping into their greatness that their life will be forever free from resistance when they reach a certain level. Is there anything agitating you right now? Is there anything moving or forcing you into violent, irregular action? Is there anything disturbing or exciting you emotionally? If not, my friend, then you are comfortable.

I have a thought that I'd like you to ponder. You've sentenced yourself to 10 years in Comfort Penitentiary, and you have a schedule that you have to follow. You're not in control of your own life, your routine is pretty much the same every day, and you're being watched and observed religiously as you serve your sentence. But, just like you locked yourself up, you have the power to set yourself free. The only reason you're in jail is because you put yourself there. You have the power to leave.

I have a dog. His name is Paco. He's deadly afraid of these two medal frames that make a terrifying noise when they're moved. He doesn't like to come near these frames. Because of this, I can give him restrictions that he'll never test purely because he's afraid of these frames. But what Paco doesn't know is that these frames are harmless. He could easily remove the restriction of these frames by purely knocking them down and walking past them. If he only overcame his fear by testing these frames, he'd know that he has nothing to fear at all.

My reason in both of these examples is to communicate that you really have nothing to fear at all. In the first example,

I want you to know that just like you have the power to lock yourself up, you also have the power to set yourself free. There's no officer on duty trying to prevent you from escaping. If there is a guard, understand that they have been employed by YOU. One's job description is to keep you in confinement and make sure you never escape. That's "Officer Fear", and you have him on salary. You could actually fire him with a stroke of your pen and hire a new guard called "Officer Imagination and Optimism". This guard's sole responsibility is to encourage you to explore what life would be like for you outside of the walls of this prison that you've created for yourself. You're the boss. You're in control of who you hire and fire.

You need to hire people in your life who are going to help you see the possibilities. They're going to encourage you to look past your fear and give you hope and faith for a future that is on the other side of your pessimism. You need people in your life who are going to speak into you. Who won't let you settle for a life in confinement, but will encourage you to test your limits? Many times when limits are tested, you realize that you have none. These are your officers. These are the friends and family members who believe in your vision and won't let you settle for less. Sometimes, it's hard to believe something you don't have a prototype for. You didn't witness anyone in your life attempting to achieve the level of success that you desire.So when times get tough, you need people (Officers) around who reassure you that you are going in the right direction. These people will embolden you to break free.

In the second example, I just need you to realize that fear is only there so that you can overcome it. YOU MUST HAVE

OBSTACLES. But don't create obstacles for yourself. Don't worry, calamity will come. You don't have to create it for yourself. Just like my dog, he created obstacles within his mind that he's forced to live within now. The confines that you've placed on yourself are oftentimes within your mind. The consequences of that fear you feel will most of the time not be manifested.

But fear in regards to pursuing your destiny is often made up scenarios in your head that never come to fruition.

This doesn't mean that fear isn't real. If you walk onto a freeway with hundreds of cars going 80 miles an hour, you're likely to be hit and seriously injured, or die. That fear is real. But fear in regards to pursuing your destiny is often made up scenarios in your head that never come to fruition. And IF they do, usually the result is never as bad as you think. You have been engineered to adapt, readjust and evolve. You won't keep failing in the same areas because it literally goes against your nature. As human beings, we're not wired to continue making the same mistakes over and over again. Eventually, for the most part, we WILL find a way.

I'm asking you to consider the possibilities. What if all of this time you haven't gone after what you really want, because comfort made you fear a consequence that will never come to pass? So, what if you fail? You'll make the necessary adjustments. What if they laugh at you? They can laugh now but you'll be the one laughing later. What I'm saying is regardless of what happens, it's all going to work out in your favor. You just have to be willing to get uncomfortable for you to manifest it.

EXPOSURE & ENVIRONMENT

Exposure - the fact of experiencing something or being affected by it because of being in a particular situation or place. In many instances, the very thing that stops you from becoming the best version of yourself is exposure. In the last chapter, we talked about putting yourself in situations that make you uncomfortable. One of the many ways you can do this is through exposure. Exposure is so critical because you only know what you've been exposed to.

I was a young boy who grew up in the hood. I had never been on an airplane. I had never known what it was like to ride in a nice car, eat at restaurants that you had to dress up to go to, or sleep peacefully without worrying about if a stray bullet would come flying through my window. Gunshots were the norm where I come from. You kind of get used to them after a while. College was something of a myth. I mean they barely mentioned college in the elementary school I attended. I know you're probably like, "But Joshua, you were in elementary school, they probably aren't telling you about college in the 4th grade." Yes they are. It just depends on the schools you attend in your environment.

In the environment I grew up in, most teachers didn't believe that most of us kids would make it out. They didn't give us hope for the future. They were just doing their jobs because somebody needed to do it. You could tell by their approach that they knew you would end up in jail, dead, or in some low-end career. For the most part, they didn't see us as kids worth saving. When you are raised in this type of environment, how can you ever have real hope for anything different? You do what you know. In most instances, you become the environment you are being exposed to. I didn't know what life was like outside of the hood because I had never seen it before, UNTIL we moved out of that environment.

Thank God for a mom who understood that her children wouldn't have the best chance at life if we stayed in that environment. I'll tell you the truth: I have always been a natural born leader, and I've always had a desire for entrepreneurship. Who do you think I would have become if I would have stayed in that environment? I can tell you, I probably would have become one of the biggest drug lords on the North East side of Houston. I was too ambitious to settle for small things. First, I would have taken the block. Then I would have taken the neighborhood. Then I would have taken the city. Next, the state, then the region. Of course, this would have only happened if I wasn't killed in the process. I've always had ambition for big things, so if I would have stayed in that environment, my ambition would never have let me be ok with selling dime sacks on the corner. I would eventually do what I was exposed to - sell dope.

You know, it's funny how people who were not raised in that kind of environment can look down or offer opinions about what someone should do who was raised in that kind of environment. These are the people who watch the news and think they have the solution to your problems. They make change sound so easy…"Those people need to work hard like I did for what they want!" "They need to stop going to jail and committing crime!" Yeah, they make it sound so easy. It's a lot more complicated than that.

I'm sure at some point of time in your life, you've heard the saying that you can't change anyone. They have to want to change for themselves. That's true to some extent, but change isn't that simple. If it were, everyone would change because who wants to voluntarily continue destructive behaviors? If it were that easy, you wouldn't have homeless people, drug addicts, habitual criminal offenders, people who are incapable of maintaining a healthy relationship, emotionless fathers, or women who can't keep healthy friendships. This list could go on for pages. The point is, if change is "so simple", wouldn't people just do it? Have you ever thought to yourself, "Why is it so hard to change bad habits or behaviors?"

The point is, if change is "so simple", wouldn't people just do it?

Do you actually think that criminals enjoy jail, that a person who is always late to work enjoys being fired, or a woman who is just trying to find love enjoys going through her third divorce? Do children enjoy getting failing grades? Naturally, people don't want to experience the negative consequences that come from their actions, but yet they can't seem to change them. If you know something's bad for you, why can't you just stop? There's a reason for this. About 70% of smokers say they would like to quit. Many of us have unhealthy excess weight that we could lose if only we would eat right and exercise more. So why don't we do it?

That's because habits are hard to break, especially when a lot of habits are formed through your personal experiences and reinforced by your environment. When we think, feel, and act in a particular way over a period of time, habits form, not only in our behavior but in our memory systems too.

...habits are hard to break, especially when a lot of habits are formed through your personal experiences and reinforced by your environment.

Albert Bandura, an American psychologist, believed that people learn behaviors by observing and modeling other people's behavior, attitudes, or emotions. In order for you to model anyone's behavior, you have to be exposed to them. You have to be within their environment. In particular, he studied babies and young children and found that they imitated the behavior of those around them. This became the foundation of his social learning theory in which he highlighted that any form of learning requires the individual's attention, retention, reproduction, and motivation to imitate the modeled behavior.

Have you heard of classical conditioning? Classical conditioning (also known as Pavlovian or respondent conditioning) is learning through association. John Watson denied completely the existence of the mind or consciousness. Though, I disagree with the former. Watson believed that all individual differences in behavior were due to different experiences of learning. He famously said:

"Give me a dozen healthy infants, well-formed, and my own specified world to bring them up in and I'll guarantee to take any one at random and train him to become any type of specialist I might select - doctor, lawyer, artist, merchant-chief and, yes, even beggar-man and thief, regardless of his talents, penchants, tendencies, abilities, vocations and the race of his ancestors" *(Watson, 1924, p. 104).*

So here's my question to you. If we've been conditioned to think how we think and respond how we respond, and if we've only modeled the behavior of the environments we were in, then would it be safe to assume that if we got exposed to different environments, we'd have a greater chance of changing and creating new behaviors?

It's much more common to repeat bad behaviors because these behaviors come naturally to us, whether consciously or subconsciously. Most people want to change regardless of what the judgmental outsiders think. It's simply just hard. From an outsider's point of view who doesn't have the same experience, it's easier to point the finger and say, "Don't they see that their actions have dire consequences...? Why don't they change?" It's challenging to change those habits if you're not aware of the other options available to you. The only way to know that there are alternative options available is through EXPOSURE.

I was a young kid who grew up in the hood until we moved to the suburbs. Thinking back on it, the home we moved into was relatively small. But at the time, that home seemed HUGE. I didn't realize that there was life outside of the hood until we moved out of the hood. Now, I was exposed to a new environment.

Do you know that when we were living in the hood, I would rarely go outside to play because of how dangerous it was. But when we moved to the suburbs, you couldn't stop me from going outside. I didn't have to worry much about being shot at or being caught in the crossfire. I was free, free to be a kid. I was also free to explore our new neighborhood and imagine all of the possibilities. The young entrepreneur in me still wanted to find a way to make my own money. So what did I do? I made a flier in Word Art, found a way to print out 25 flyers, and walked around my neighborhood going door-to-door trying to convince people to let me mow their lawns and wash their clothes. I was 12 at the time. I would have never done this in my old neighbor because going outside was much too dangerous. Fifty dollars wasn't enough to kill for, but it was enough to catch a brutal beating for and they didn't play fair. I would watch people get seriously beaten in my front yard with bats, chains, brass knuckles, and more. Often time, over money and respect. I could never protect myself from a fully grown man attacking me, I wouldn't stand a chance.

See, when you expose yourself to new environments, you're able to experience new possibilities. You never know what's blocking your vision when you're blinded by your environment. There could be fears holding you back that only exist within a certain setting. If you change your setting, maybe you wouldn't have the same fears. The only way to truly know is to change your setting. I know this sounds simple but it's not.

For example, let's say that you're the first person in your family to ever graduate college. I would make the assumption that you would have to overcome certain challenges and mental roadblocks that you probably didn't know existed within you. Maybe you have a fear of success because of how your friends and family might view you if you were successful. Will they think that you think you're too good now? Will they think that you're stuck up? Will they make certain remarks that are shameful and make you feel little as a college graduate? Or maybe it's the opposite, maybe you wear the pressure of success on your shoulders. If you don't graduate, not only have you failed yourself, but you've failed the people who were counting on you as well. You're the catalyst for a new generation for generations to come. That level of pressure can be crushing at times.

If you didn't grow up in the environment of success, failure feels comfortable.

If you didn't grow up in the environment of success, failure feels comfortable. It would be much easier for you not to attend college and succumb to the very life you are trying to escape, than it would to triumph and crush all of your goals. It's always harder to change than it is to stay the same, especially if that's all you know.

Not only that, you don't have people around you who can reinforce new behaviors by speaking life into you. They are shackled by their limited experience as well. Graduating college may be a huge obstacle for them, something that they've never even considered. So how can they ever sincerely convince you that you can complete it? What if you decided to stop going, what do you likely think would be their response? They might try to talk you out of it, encourage you to keep pressing forward but that energy won't last because they themselves have not tasted success to communicate with conviction the necessity of crossing the finish line.

But on the contrary, what if you did grow up in an environment where success and prosperity were typical? Your parents were successful. Your grandparents were successful. Your uncle and aunt were successful. Your older siblings were successful. What do you think would subconsciously happen for you? Since you have the benefit of being exposed to a blueprint, a prototype, your chances of success will likely increase dramatically. Why? Because success is the norm for you. You were born, bred, and cultivated in the environment of success, so it's almost second nature for you now. That's all you know. It's all you've been exposed to. That can come with pressure, sure, but you've been conditioned to handle that pressure because you've gotten a chance to witness being raised in an environment where overcoming is the norm.

I always say that people who have had the benefit of growing up in a home with both parents have the advantage when it comes to co-existing in a successful relationship. I'm not saying that their parents' relationship was perfect. I'm sure, like every relationship, it had its challenges that these people had to overcome. But that's the beauty of it. These two individuals found a way to overcome those challenges all while their children are watching from afar. Being a child who grew up in a home where both parents worked through conflict, learned how to effectively communicate with each other, and ultimately selflessly love each other gives that child a giant edge over someone who was raised in a single parent home. They purely have the advantage because they've been exposed to it.

This is why being exposed to new environments is so critical for your growth and development.

In combination with growing up in the hood, going to church was a huge part of my development. I grew up in Pentecostal, Baptist, Methodist, COGIC, and Non-denominational churches. I guess you could say that I was cultured when it comes to my church experience. My dad and step-dad were pastors, and my mom was/is a prophet/minister. I grew up in a church where people "cut a rug" and would "take a lap" at a moment's notice. (You had to have grown up in church yourself to understand these references, lol.) If you've ever been to a traditionally Black church, then you know what you wear to church is just as important as the singing. It's just as important as the preaching. You wouldn't dare come to church dressed any kind of way. The men must be groomed and the women must be modest. If your dress was too short, the ushers would politely/aggressively offer you a sheet to cover up those legs.

One of the popular things that men wore to church at that time were suits that had 8-10 buttons on them. I mean, these suits would be in various colors too. Some could be gold, others could be purple, green, or pink. Depending on the occasion, you always broke out your best. Once I was ordained as a minister and preacher, I wanted to impress my other colleagues by getting a suit that would turn heads. The first suit I got was a cream -golden suit. It was cream with golden stitching. I can't lie, it was fly at the time. I was feeling myself. It had a vest that had 4-5 buttons on it, and a blazer that had 8-10 buttons on it. When I walked into church, I just knew it would turn heads and let everyone know that I'm not to be played with. I was proud of my golden suit.

And then...

I started going to college. The college world was much different than the church world. If I had worn my golden suit to college, I would have gotten odd looks from my peers. I'm sure some of them would have laughed at me and talked about me amongst themselves, as I strutted down the courtyard thinking I was the flyest thing since sliced bread. I'm sure they would have been thinking..."Why is this young dude walking around here dressed like an old MAN?!" Though my suit was ok in one environment, it would have gotten me ridiculed in another environment.

I didn't know this at the time, but purely by attending college, I was exposing myself to a new environment. The culture was different in this environment. It was outside of my norm, therefore, it inherently made me uncomfortable. Usually, fear tries to attach itself to new things. See, I was "the man" in my last environment. I had built a level of authority and credibility in my church environment. But in college, I was no one. No one knew me. No one respected me. No one cared who I was. And unfortunately,my golden suit didn't impress them.

In the last chapter, I talked about overcoming your comfort. Can you imagine how uncomfortable I was in this new environment? No one wanted to hear me preach nor were they impressed with my ability to quote scripture. The affirmation, applause, and notoriety that came from my church environment didn't exist in college. I was nobody. It made me completely uncomfortable. That's usually what will happen when you get exposed to new things. The reason most people don't want to expose themselves to new experiences is because many times it will flatten their ego. Exposing yourself to new experiences will humble you. Maybe you have to start over. Maybe what worked for you then isn't going to work for you now. Maybe your expertise over there doesn't apply over here. And, maybe you have to realize that you're not really all that and you've got a lot to learn - and that's a hit to your pride.

Driving a box truck is not the same as driving an 18-wheeler. Anyone with a regular driver's license can drive a box truck. But driving an 18-wheeler requires another level of skill and expertise. It can also be intimidating to drive an 18-wheeler because the risks associated with driving an 18-wheeler are greater. Mistakes are different at this level. If you crash a box truck you could injure or maybe even kill someone depending on the circumstance. But, if your 18-wheeler trailer and truck flip over on the freeway, you could cause an explosion, a multi car pile up, and multiple casualties, not to mention the client product that you're transporting is ruined forever. There's more on the line when you're driving an 18-wheeler. The level of risk is different. You have to be willing to accept everything that comes with going to the next level, because everything is greater...greater failure...greater collapse...greater defeat...greater frustration...greater wins. But you can't accept greater wins without acknowledging greater losses.

I'm saying that to say that exposure to another level will make you uncomfortable. There's a reason why that is. I had a choice to make. I could either choose to shrink back and succumb to my pride and ego, play it small, and be defeated by my insecurities, or I could accept this as a new challenge that I had to adapt and overcome if I wanted to go to my next level. Needless to say, college changed me.

I wasn't the most respected person in the room. I wasn't the smartest person in the room and I needed help in areas that I didn't know I needed help in, until I exposed myself to a different environment that made me feel insecure.

I soon realized that my golden suit would not suffice in this new environment. But here's the thing, I also had to accept the fact that I didn't really know how to dress. This was a hit to my ego and self-image. It made me think that I wasn't enough. That what I had accomplished so far meant nothing. There's no way that the "golden boy" didn't know how to dress. When I was in high school, I could wear white tees and air force ones and I was the man. Now that I'm in my twenties in college, I just looked like I was from the hood because every person from the ghetto wore that. I had to step it up. It was a hard reality to face when I came to the conclusion that I didn't know how to dress. But now I must adapt and conquer. This is a challenge for me and I'm up for the challenge.

Most people don't like to expose themselves to new environments because of how challenging it can be for them. New challenges are often intimating.

Most people don't like to expose themselves to new environments because of how challenging it can be for them. New challenges are often intimating. But there's no way around new challenges if you want to become who you were born to be. I had to make new friends. I had to get around people who were smarter than me, who were more experienced than me, and who knew a thing or two about how to navigate in this new environment. To even make steps in that direction, I had to come to a place where I humbled myself.

Have you ever heard of bibliophobia? It is an intense fear of books or reading. It's a type of anxiety disorder. People with bibliophobia may experience shame or embarrassment about reading. They may get nervous when they merely think about books. They might panic when they have to read a book and they completely avoid it because it intimidates them. It makes them have to acknowledge their inadequacies and their deficiencies. They have to acknowledge that they are not as great as they think they are. Therefore, they never learn how to read because they're afraid of how not knowing how to read will make them feel.

People have phobias when it comes to exposing themselves to new things that challenge them. They spend their entire life avoiding it because of the feelings that are associated with experiencing it - I'm not good enough,I'm not smart enough,

I don't speak well enough. These are just some of the things we tell ourselves when we're faced with recognizing our short-comings. But if you only knew how much embracing exposure to new environments could truly change your life.

Sure, I didn't like how not knowing how to dress and feeling completely out of my element made me feel. But I was able to overcome those feelings because what was ahead of me was greater than what was behind me. I didn't want to hold on to the back door while trying to go out the front door. But when I let go of the back door, I was able to enter into my next. I wasn't confident. I was nervous. But I was determined.

So how did I adjust to this new environment called college life? I found a group of friends who were a part of this male organization that was making a lot of noise on campus. They seemed prestigious. They had mentorship and connections on campus. This organization intrigued me, they had what I lacked. These men dressed differently. They were motivated, smart, and prudent leaders. They could be the catalyst to my next level. I got involved with the organization and started to develop new friendships. They introduced me to the finer things in life. They exposed me to GQ magazine. They exposed me to the executive leadership on campus, and also allowed me to sit in on board meetings. I got a chance to observe their mannerisms and how they carried themselves. They taught me how to conduct myself when I got into the room.

I learned a lot from being a part of this organization. As I continued to build my relationships with these brothers, an opportunity became available for me to run for a leadership position on the board. I leaped at this opportunity because I knew that I had established the network, trust, hustle, and connections I needed to win. I won the position by large demand and my confidence, as well as my style (wink wink), had now gone to another level.

I would not have won this position had I not conquered my insecurities and self-doubt. Self-doubt can be sneaky. It can creep up on you at a moment's notice and completely take you by surprise. But that's normal. If you show me someone who has never dealt with self-doubt, I'll show you someone who has probably spent most of their life in the "safe zone". People who play it "safe" never really have to worry about doubting themselves because they are comfortable with what they know and don't care to push their boundaries.

If you show me someone who has never dealt with self-doubt, I'll show you someone who has probably spent most of their life in the "safe zone"

Exposure for your next level is a game changer. Look, you don't know what you don't know until you're exposed to it. I didn't know that fire would burn me until I touched fire. I didn't know that heights weren't that bad until I rode my first roller coaster. What was funny about my first roller coaster experience is that my older brother knew it was my first time.

As we waited in line until it was our turn, he would say things like, "You ready?" "Are you sure you want to do this?" "This isn't for wimps...". He went on and on, but I was determined. The rollercoaster was called, "The Batman", and there was a huge splash of red paint on the railing. Can you guess what he told me when he saw the red paint? He told me that someone had fallen to their death recently and that was their blood on the railing, lol. My heart dropped. "So you're telling me that I could die on this roller coaster..." is what I thought to myself. Nevertheless I pressed forward, stricken by fear, only to be made aware that it was red paint the entire time.

Our life is full of little wins and losses like this. You may look at the small areas in your life where you've succumbed to fear and think, "Oh, it's not a big deal." When in actuality, it's a huge deal. Small losses become big losses. Small wins become big wins. If you find that you've talked yourself out of little things over your life span, I can guarantee you that as an adult you've most likely talked yourself out of bigger opportunities as well. The most disheartening thing about this is that in the end you realize that it was all in your head. Your fear was unjustified.

So the question is how do you expose yourself to new environments? Well, I need you to know something first: humans can adapt to many different environments. We can survive in cold and hot environments, different climates, and even different habitats. We can survive in cold environments because we have a thick layer of fat under our skin to keep us warm. Humans also have hair on their heads that keeps them warm by trapping heat in their bodies. This helps humans live in cold areas of the world like Alaska, where temperatures are very low all year round.

Humans can also survive in hot environments because they sweat and their skin is good at absorbing the water from sweat, so it evaporates quickly from their skin and cools their body temperature, especially when it's very hot outside (like in the desert). We also have hair to keep us warm, as well as block UV light exposure. Humans are able to adapt because they have the flexibility to eat, learn from others, live in different environments, and make and use tools.

You may not have thought of yourself like this, but I need you to know that you were literally born for this. You could have been a fly. You could have been a dog. You could have been a bird. But no, you entered this world as a human. I need you to understand how much of an advantage that is. I need you to appreciate and not squander the opportunity you've been given. There's nothing too complex that's been presented to you that you cannot overcome. We've been doing it since the beginning of time. How do you think we got here today? From traveling on horses to flying on planes, we've adapted and evolved. You were born to adapt to any environment you go into.

I need you to intentionally expose yourself to new challenging environments. I need you to ask yourself, "What intimidates me?"

So here's what I need you to do. I need you to intentionally expose yourself to new challenging environments. I need you to ask yourself, "What intimidates me?" That's a good place to start. Start with the things you talk yourself out of doing. Start with the opportunities your reasoned yourself out of. "I don't have the degree, they'll never hire me...why apply?" Your reasoning is valid. I get it. You looked at the application and they said that you need 3 years of experience and a Master's in communications. You don't have a master's in communication so you figure that you could never get the job, YOU DON'T QUALIFY. That's a reasonable assumption to make. But it's an assumption nonetheless. That assumption prevents you from taking action. The real fear that you have is the fear of being rejected. That's what you're really running from. You're running from the feeling that you'll feel if they say, "sorry, but we decided to go with another candidate."

Because you don't want to feel this feeling of rejection, you don't even make the attempt. You only apply for positions that you qualify for. Why? Because it's comfortable. But what if you did apply? What if you challenged yourself and decided to be relentless? What if you said to yourself that someone is going to hire you in this position whether you're qualified or not? What if you started to actually believe that any company that passed up on you would be losing one of the greatest candidates for their company that they've ever seen? What if you actually believe this stuff about you?

Can you imagine what lengths you would go to if you started to radically believe that you were capable of anything?

Can you imagine what lengths you would go to if you started to radically believe that you were capable of anything? So you don't apply for this job because you believe that you don't qualify; but what if you believed that you did qualify, and you refused to take no for an answer? To what lengths would you go? What level of potential would you tap into? If you started to radically believe in yourself and you were dedicated to getting the job that they say you don't qualify for, listen to me closely...NO ONE could stop you from getting that job. Why? Because your ingenuity and adaptability would start to kick in. You would find ways to outperform any candidate and make it hard for them to say no to you. See, most people would just give up. They'd read the job brief and as soon as they saw that they didn't meet certain criteria, they would move on to the next application, settling for comfort.

But if you believed that NOBODY ELSE could perform better than you in this role, you're just not going to accept no for an answer. You're going to learn about the company. You're going to learn about networking events that the company may be involved with. You're going to attend events and make connections with people who are affiliated with the company. You're going to connect with some of the employees on LinkedIn and start building relationships with them. You're going to go above and beyond to start positioning yourself as the authority on the topic that they're hiring for so this company sees you as the clear choice. You're going to record a professional video and send the hiring manager a "video resume" introducing yourself, sharing your passion for the company and how you can be an asset to the organization. If they don't respond, you're going to send another professional video finding a specific problem that the position they're hiring for solves and you solve that problem in the demo video. You would show them how you'd adapt and solve the problem that you were hired for.

You see what I mean? When you want something, you will literally go above and beyond to get it. Now tell me, if you were the hiring manager and you met this person at your company event and your colleagues told you about a great candidate they met at a networking event.... This person sent you two personalized professional videos and followed up relentlessly to show their passion for the position at your company...who's the clear winner when this hiring manager starts to look at the mountain of resumes that are sitting on their desk? It's YOU. Now tell me this, if you did this for 10 companies with the same position opening, you wouldn't get at least half of these companies to interview you? You're the clear candidate. How many other candidates do you think are going through such lengths to get this company's attention? Not even ONE PERCENT of them.

You think this hiring manager cares that you don't have a master's in communications? You've shown them that you do have a master's in communications, it's just not on paper.

If you did, all of these companies would be in bidding wars trying to get you to pick them. They don't care about what's on that paper. They only care that the person they hired is competent enough to do the job and you've proven that.There isn't any competition.

See, what I've come to realize is people give up too soon and they don't try hard enough.

You were willing to expose yourself and go the extra mile, therefore you reap the benefits. See, what I've come to realize is people give up too soon and they don't try hard enough. It's because they're crippled with fear, and they really haven't tapped into the potential that lives on the inside of them. As a human being, you've literally been forged to thrive in any environment. Why are you running from who you truly are?

I really need you to think about exposing yourself to environments that make you uncomfortable, and I need you to force yourself to live in those environments. Don't just visit those environments. Don't just take a vacation to those environments, knowing that once your vacation is over you get to go back to the comfort of what you were used to before. Sail to the environment that makes you uncomfortable, and then, burn the ships. When you burn the ships, you destroy every opportunity you have to go back. There is no going back. It's either you conquer where you are, or you die trying. It's either victory or death. (Figuratively of course, ;)

This is the mentality you need, because I think that the reason you haven't gotten to where you want to be is because you haven't gotten many chances to experience who you truly can become first-hand. You haven't witnessed you overcome obstacles time and time and time again. Because if you did, you'd rid yourself of this inconsequential fear. Exposure and new environments are the key to breaking into your future. You were built for this. You were born for this. It's time to expose yourself to your next level.

CHAPTER 7

FINDING YOUR CONFIDENCE

**CONFIDENCE - A FEELING OF SELF-
ASSURANCE ARISING FROM ONE'S APPRECI-
ATION OF ONE'S OWN ABILITIES OR
QUALITIES.**

Confidence - a feeling of self-assurance arising from one's appreciation of one's own abilities or qualities. Let me ask you a question, and I want you to pause and reflect on the question before giving your answer. I know your knee-jerk reaction to this question would have you immediately respond to it out of the embarrassment that comes from giving the wrong answer, but be honest with yourself and take your time. The question is...are you confident?

No, for real, are you really confident? We know what technically should be the right answer to this question. The right answer should be, "Yes, of course I'm confident!" God forbid you're in a crowded room of people and the speaker asks everyone who has confidence in themself to stand up, and you're one of the only ones who stay seated. The pressure from the embarrassment alone would make you stand even though you know you always second guess yourself, and you know that you are not fully confident in your abilities. But rest easy. You're not in a crowded room full of people, so you don't have to worry about what anyone will think of you if you don't stand up. You can be honest with me and yourself right now. Do you have 100% confidence in yourself and your abilities? Are you 100% sure of yourself? If so, then why has it taken you so long, huh? Why haven't you started walking in your true purpose?

It takes someone who is humble and has a high level of self-awareness to humbly admit that in some of the most scary areas of their life, they lack confidence.

It takes someone who is humble and has a high level of self-awareness to humbly admit that in some of the most scary areas of their life, they lack confidence. I'm sure you have confidence in the areas of your life that you've become familiar with. I mean, that's one of the things that keep you there - the familiarity. You're confident here because you've been doing whatever that is for a long time. You've built confidence in this area. But in other areas, areas that challenge you to go beyond what's recognizable, that's when the fear of the unknown cripples you from taking action and you need confidence to take action. This is where uncertainty and doubt creep in.

...confidence isn't the absence of doubt. It's the will to press through in the midst of doubt.

Look, confidence isn't the absence of doubt. It's the will to press through in the midst of doubt. Most people are crippled by their doubt and therefore hinder themselves from ever growing in confidence. Every time you press through in the midst of your doubt, it just builds more confidence within you. Where does your lack of confidence come from? Fear and submission to your doubt.

Let me ask you something. Would you ever follow someone who wasn't confident? I mean, you could see it in their posture, you could hear the fear, uncertainty, and weakness in their voice when they spoke. You could tell that they were not 100% convinced of what they were saying. Would you confidently follow this person? Would stake it all on their vision and put your life on hold to follow someone who was timid, who always hesitated before they made a decision and second guessed themselves?

Sure, you might give them the benefit of the doubt the first few times you pick up on their lack of confidence, but after a while, would you be able to continuously, without question, confidently follow someone who was fearful and apprehensive most of the time? Wouldn't that make you uneasy? You'd probably lose enthusiasm overtime when it comes to following such a person. Why is that? Why is it that we as human beings just won't follow someone unless they are convinced that come hell or high water, this will work? Everyone wants to follow a hopeful, optimistic, and unshakable leader. No one wants to follow an unassertive, jittery, shy, self-critical leader.

So if lacking confidence was ok, then why would most people not follow a person like that? For most of us, dealing with a confident person helps assure us that this individual is also competent. People don't follow people who show uncertainty and anxiety because fear is contagious. If you're the leader and you're always in a state of constant panic, what message do you think this is going to send the people following you? So, if you wouldn't follow someone like this, why would it ever be ok for you to lack confidence in yourself?

Do you want to know where your lack of confidence stems from? It's not the fear of the certain, it's the fear of the uncertain.

Do you want to know where your lack of confidence stems from? It's not the fear of the certain, it's the fear of the uncertain. Do you remember the first time you watched your favorite movie? Did it have you on the edge of your seat? Did you cry? Did you clench? Did you cover your eyes because you didn't want to see what was going to happen next? Did you laugh uncontrollably? Now think about the second time you watched the movie, did you have those same emotions the second time around? Probably not because you had already seen the movie. You know what's going to happen next. Though you may enjoy it, you don't experience the same emotion you experienced when you watched it the first time around. Why is this the case? Because you're certain of how things will play out.

Certainty is self-affirming. That's why we don't need validation or applause from people when we are certain. I'm sure there are areas in your life where you are certain. Maybe you've been working your job for 5 years and you know it like the back of your hand. Maybe you've been a mom of two for 8 years, so the thought of having another child doesn't bring as much anxiety as it did when you had your first child. Maybe you've always excelled in math and science. Maybe you've always been a trustworthy friend, and maybe you've always been outgoing, so new environments with new people don't make you nervous. It's easier to be certain when you've developed a routine, when you've been doing something for so long that it doesn't challenge you anymore. But it's harder to be certain, free from doubt or reservation, in the midst of uncertainty.

The confidence you need for your next level is going to be built through uncertainty.

The confidence you need for your next level is going to be built through uncertainty. This is because what you're about to experience, you haven't experienced before. Therefore, it will make you uneasy. It's new and fresh, therefore uncertainty will creep in. If you stop pressing forward because you feel uncertain, you'll never go to the next level. Most people perceive uncertainty as a red flag. They view uncertainty as a dead end, and what do you do when you get to dead ends? You turn around and go back in the direction you came. Uncertainty isn't a dead end, it's a new beginning. It's a new opportunity. Sure, there isn't a defined path already laid before you. But there is ground to create the path. You just have to be able to see the opportunities. Just because you have hit a dead end doesn't mean that you shouldn't go in that direction. It might just mean that your car can't go down this path. You might have to get out of your car and go on foot. You might have to go to your local hardware store, buy an ax, come back to that dead end and start cutting down trees to forge a path for yourself.

You build confidence for the next phase of your life by pressing through doubt and fear, and overcoming your uncertainty.

You build confidence for the next phase of your life by pressing through doubt and fear, and overcoming your uncertainty. You may have never cut down a tree a day in your life, so the very thought of having to chop down trees to forge your own path is overwhelming. It's daunting. Look at all of those trees! It's going to take you forever - years to create a path. You don't have any skills in this area. And if you're honest, you'd rather not. It would be much easier to just find another way around. Maybe you could catch a plane to the other side. But unfortunately, going to the next level of your destiny doesn't quite work like that. There are always going to be obstacles in your way and unfortunately, there is no other way around. You have to go through them.

I remember when I was playing football in middle school. The coach would have us get into the pit. What's the pit? The pit is where all the players would circle around 2 players who had to go head-to-head. The player who tackled the other was the winner. There was no way "around" your opponent, the coach said. You either go through them, or you risk being defeated. Everyone wants to "go around" their greatest obstacle. But what you don't understand is that persevering through hardship is the best way to find your confidence. Think about it. When you conquer interference, when you overcome something that you didn't think you could overcome, how does it make you feel? Do you feel empowered? Do you feel like if you can beat this you can beat anything? Do you feel accomplished? Do you feel proud? I'm sure you probably feel all of those things and more. Experiencing all of these emotions can only lead to one result:more confidence. But if you've spent the entirety of your life taking the easy way around, then you've robbed yourself from the beauty of these emotions.

I want to tell you a little secret. Let's say you were at a dead end and you did try to take another way around, figuratively speaking. You hopped on a plane and just flew over. Here's what would happen when you landed; you would get off of the plane only to realize there is another dead end. You'd probably think to yourself, "Now wait a minute! I thought I just flew over the other dead end, there's another one?!" Then you jumped back on the plane and flew over that dead end only to land and see another. And the cycle repeats itself. Why am I telling you this? Because it doesn't matter how many times you try to avoid doing the hard work. Every time you're getting ready to elevate you're going to hit what seems to be a dead end. You're either going to turn around and go back, or you're going to waste time trying to go around and avoid it. Or you're going to pick up an ax and GO THROUGH IT. There's no other option. Your confidence depends on it.

Practical Steps on Finding Your Confidence

STEP 1: Practice Makes Confidence

My son started playing football last year. He really loves the game of football. It's funny because he's small like me when I was that age. Because of our smaller stature, it naturally doesn't give us an edge on the football field. Size matters. After the football season was over, he expressed his enjoyment for the game and how he was looking forward to next season. He was so pumped that we even tried to go join another football league, but unfortunately the kids were much smaller than him in size, so it wouldn't have been any competition for him. So during the spring and summer, I noticed something. When my son would come home, he would either jump on the game and play Fortnite with his friends, or he would jump on his laptop and play Roadblocks with his cousins. He never spent much time practicing football.

It was kind of weird to me, because in my generation, we were always outside and rarely on the game. But this generation is different. They spend most of their time playing Xbox or Playstation. I realized that even though he liked to play football, he didn't have the desire to be the best. Maybe he lacked confidence. So one day, I told him to get off of the game and let's talk. I asked him, "Son, what was one of the reasons that you think you made the B team?" The first thing he cited was his size. He felt like he was better than a few people that made the A team, but because they were bigger, they chose to go with them over him. Because he knew his size would be a factor going into the next year, I think he knew he probably wouldn't make the A team.

So next year came around and football season was upon us once again. He tried out again and he was disappointed because he didn't make the A team...again. I had to be honest with my son at this point, because when I asked him why he didn't make it, he cited his size again. Last year was his first year so I let him make it with that excuse, but this year I would keep it real with him. I told him, "Son, the reason you didn't make the A team has nothing to do with your size. The reason you didn't make the A team is because you weren't good enough." His countenance had fallen when I said that. I wasn't trying to make him any sadder than he already was, but this was a time for a teachable moment. I had to instill this core value, this core principle in him. I told him, "Son, the reason you didn't make the A team is because you didn't practice enough. You spent most of your spring and summer playing the game. You improved over the year through natural growth and athleticism, but you didn't grow leaps and bounds because you never spent your time building your confidence through PRACTICE."

He agreed with me. The benefit of practice is that practice helps you build confidence. The reason you're not confident in whatever your specialty is is purely because you just haven't done it enough. Practice builds muscle memory. Muscle memory builds confidence. The reason most people suck when it's game time is because they haven't developed muscle memory through practice. Then, when it's time to play the game, they're nervous and in their head because they're not confident, and subsequently implode.

Muscle memory is the ability to reproduce a particular movement without conscious thought, acquired as a result of frequent repetition of that movement. The reason you're not good is not because you're not good. Does that make sense? You just haven't practiced enough. You haven't had enough reps to become proficient and confident in what you do. If we take chopping down trees as an example... chopping down trees is hard but if I did it enough not only would it become easier, I would become more confident because but I would find a way to do it faster. I would adapt and become more proficient at it. This is what happens when you practice.

How often do you practice on your dreams? Do you spend a considerable amount of systematic time honing in on your purpose and building your confidence?

I want you to ask yourself something, and you must be honest with your answer. How often do you practice on your dreams? Do you spend a considerable amount of systematic time honing in on your purpose and building your confidence? Or, do your dreams get your leftovers? Do your dreams get the bare minimum? If you spend most of your time practicing on someone else's dream and wondering why you haven't built the confidence to go after your own, therein lies the answer. For some of you, the reason you're not confident is because you haven't had enough practice.

Practice also helps you overcome self. Yep. One of the main things stopping you is you - self-sabotaging behaviors, self sabotaging thoughts; thoughts like, "I'm not good enough". "I'm not experienced enough." "I don't have the right qualifi-cations." "I feel like an imposter, who am I to do something like this?" "It's going to fail, and when it does, what will people think about me?" or "People won't take me seriously."

All of these things that you're thinking are talking yourself out of your purpose. But practice can help you overcome self. While practicing, you start to develop confidence. You start to develop muscle memory. So when it's game time, sure you will lose some, but that works in your favor. Losses turn into lessons. Even a loss is just practice for a BIG win. Too many people focus on their losses instead of their wins. It's all about perspective.

Did you know that most record labels sign a bunch of artists every year? And guess what, most of these artists flop. But does the record label care if they flop? No. Why? Because they know if they sign enough artists one of them is going to hit and when that one hits, the return on investment for that one artist is going to make up for all the other artists that flopped. You have to realize that when you're living your purpose, you have now entered the big league of life.

When you're in the big league, you have to take BIG RISKS...

...More on this later.

See, you're too focused on what you're going to lose versus the fact that if you put in enough reps, you're going to win. And when you do, it's going to make up for every loss. You're going to hit it BIG. Don't get so set on the potential of losing that you decide not to show up for practice. Because practice is going to build the confidence to persevere past every mental block that's going to try and stop you from pushing forward. Practice where you're going to get your confidence to continue.

I want you to know that you cannot "wing" practice. Practice has to be intentional. If you have an "I'll get to it when I get to it" type of attitude, you'll never make the time to practice on your purpose. I need you to do something right now. I need you to schedule intentional time for you to practice on your purpose. If your purpose is to write scripts for major films, I need you to buy the screenplay software and start writing, even if you don't know where to start. It's like chopping down the tree. Even though you don't have experience at chopping down a tree, the only way to learn is to start chopping, not by researching how to chop. That's what most people do, they research their way into mediocre. The reason they do this is because they think that research is work. Research is research. Work is work. Don't ever confuse the two.

Many times, excessive research is just a reason to procrastinate - masked as perfectionism. The reason you spend your time doing so much research is because you're a perfectionist that's afraid of failure. Research is your way of procrastinating. Don't give yourself a pat on the back because you've compiled pages and pages of research. That's nothing to be excited about. Research is one thing, doing the work is another. So many people practice on research instead of practicing on their purpose, then wonder why they still feel stuck. confused, asking themselves, "Why haven't I made much progress?" It's because research is not equal work. Sooner or later, you're going to have to stop running from doing, and actually DO the work.

Isn't it funny how habitual researchers have the audacity to tell doers how it should be done? Google has emboldened procrastinators. They've watched the videos, studied the training, even bought the books. But what they don't have is real world experience. It's like Mike Tyson said, "Everyone has a plan until they get punched in the face." To develop plans can be fulfilling and unfulfilling at the same time. It's fulfilling because developing the plan makes you feel like you're making progress. But if you never execute on the plan, then it is just a bunch of exquisite words on paper. Plans are useless without execution. Spend more time on practice than you do on your plans.

Plans are useless without execution. Spend more time on practice than you do on your plans.

Real practice should ALWAYS feel like the real thing. Can you practice chopping down a tree without actually chopping down a tree? No, you can not. See, procrastinators believe that just because they've researched the technique of how to chop down trees faster, they know how to chop down the tree even though they've never done it before. While they spend time on their mobile phones researching all the best techniques, a guy like me is actually in the forest with my ax learning from first hand experience. There are going to be things that I learn from REAL WORLD practice that I would never learn from research. There are going to be some questions that you just don't know to ask until you actually start doing it. Don't ever confuse research with practice.

Practice is what's going to build your confidence. The greatest reason why is because you're going to learn better techniques along the way. You're wired to acclimate as a human being so you will adapt, overcome, and get better. This is one of the greatest ways to build confidence, so if you don't have confidence, I'm almost 100% percent sure that the reason why is because you just haven't had enough practice.

STEP 2: Take Risks with Major Consequences

I need you to know that every risk isn't the same. Why is that? Because every risk doesn't have an equal consequence. If I run a stop sign and get caught by the police, they may give me a ticket and I'll have to pay a fine. If I run a stop sign going 90 miles per hour and kill two people, they're not going to let me off with a ticket. Because lives were lost, the consequence is much more severe. Am I saying that you should take big risks by disobeying the law, running stop signs at 100 miles per hour? No. What I'm saying is that most people spend their lives taking small risks expecting BIG rewards, and it doesn't work like that. Small risks equal meager rewards. Big risks equal bigger rewards.

Small risks equal meager rewards. Big risks equal bigger rewards.

The adverse is true as well. Small risks equal small consequences. Big risks equal bigger consequences. If you jump off of a one-story building, you likely won't be hurt or break your leg. You likely won't have to go to the hospital for a major injury. Now if you were pushed off of a one-story building, that may be a different story. I used to jump from the roof of my one-story home all the time as a kid, and I was never injured. But just because I was never injured jumping off of a one-story building as a kid, does not mean that I would not be injured if I jumped out of a plane flying 10,000 feet in the sky. The consequences are far different. It would be foolish of me to compare the two. One, there's barely a chance that I could even injure myself. The other, I could die.

Most people take small risks because they're playing it safe. If things don't pan out the way they planned, the consequence experienced from their failed attempt is trivial. It's inconsequential.

Most people take small risks because they're playing it safe. If things don't pan out the way they planned, the consequence experienced from their failed attempt is trivial. It's inconsequential. But if they take a HUGE risk, the consequences experienced could be significant. Therefore, it's easier to play it safe because there aren't major repercussions involved.

The problem with how most people assess risks is they rarely assess risks while looking at the entire picture. They typically only think about the negative consequences of them going, but they fail to see that there are negative consequences associated with them staying as well. Let's say that as a married person, you weren't fulfilled at your current job. You feel stuck. You've hit a ceiling, and lost your enthusiasm. At this point, you're just going to work. You want to leave your job but you can't. Why? Both you and your spouse's income help to cover the expenses. If you sporadically left your job, that would put your family in a dire position financially. Maybe you're not able to maintain the lifestyle you've grown accustomed to. Maybe you lose your home, your car, and our way of living. Those are serious consequences that have to be taken into consideration before making a move like that. I understand.

However, have you assessed the risks of you staying at your current job? Have you thought about those consequences as well - the less time you would have with your loved ones, how unhappy you would be, how resentful you would become, and how that resentment would eventually end your marriage? Have you thought about you being stuck there for another 5 years, losing more time and opportunity, coincidentally giving up on your purpose? Have you thought about how your life would lack meaning and what it would be like for you to live a life full of regret? You might be thinking to yourself, "Well, at least I won't lose my home...." That's true, but then a pandemic hits and you end up being laid off anyway. Then you realize how much you really aren't in control of your life anyway. There are always risks and consequences for both decisions. Most people spend their life trying to reduce risks as much as possible, simultaneously trapping themselves in the safe zone.

If you really want to become who you were born to be, you can't continue to take risks that play it safe. You have to challenge yourself by taking risks that have real consequences.

If you really want to become who you were born to be, you can't continue to take risks that play it safe. You have to challenge yourself by taking risks that have real consequences. This isn't to say that you shouldn't exercise wisdom in your decision making. I just need you to know that with what you're trying to achieve in life, you'll need to step out on the ledge at some point. With where you're trying to go, it's going to take faith. And faith doesn't know what's going to happen at every turn. Faith is risky. If you're not ready to take some serious risks to obtain the life you want, you'll probably never have the life you want.

STEP 3: Prayer & Guidance

I identify as a Christian, so prayer is a huge part of my journey. Prayer keeps me centered. Prayer calms me. Prayer settles my spirit. Prayer lets me know that everything is going to be ok even when I'm feeling anxious. Prayer helps me to keep going even when I feel like giving up. Prayer gives me the confidence to keep pushing forward when I feel like giving up. When I start second guessing myself and have moments where I feel like turning back, prayer settles my heart and keeps me focused. It isn't an understatement to say that prayer is a huge part of my life. Prayer is a huge part of my confidence.

I believe that I'm here for a greater purpose. I submit my life to a Higher Being, the One who created me and has given me a reason for living. I truly believe that my life is not my own. I'm here to serve people - to serve you. And prayer helps me to stay aligned with my destiny. I'll be honest with you. There are LOTS of times where I don't feel confident, where I second guess myself, and where I feel like I've made the wrong decision. But there's something about praying to Someone who is greater than me who already has it all figured out. I get a sense of peace from that because I know that it will all work out how it's supposed to. I do what I can do, and then I let God handle the rest. Without prayer and my relationship with Him, I wouldn't have confidence. I would be overcome with selfish ambition and feel lost.

I need you to know that whatever it is that you're supposed to do, with that leap of faith that you need to take, you're going to need confidence in yourself to do it. When I survey my life, I'm almost positive that without confidence I would have never become who I was born to be. For me, developing confidence was so critical because what do you do when people don't believe in you? When they sneer at your dreams, they scoff underneath their breath, don't support you, or ask you questions that make you second guess your decision? What do you do then? I'll tell you. You will need confidence in yourself to overcome their pessimism, as well as you will need confidence to overcome the pessimism that you have going on in your own head as well.

The battlefield for your purpose is more mental than it is physical. The battle you're in for the life you want is fought on two fronts. You're fighting against the negative things you tell yourself, and you're fighting against the people who say they support you but secretly hope that you don't succeed. You can feel that they don't want you to triumph even though they'll never say it. You see it in their actions. How will you overcome the enemy within and without? You will need unshakable confidence, unshakeable belief in what you're called to do and undying perseverance to see it through. It's already in you, it's time for it to be awakened.

CONQUERING DESTRUCTIVE COMPARISON

Man, man, man! In my opinion. This might be one of the most impactful chapters in this book. My goal is to hopefully unlock the unflustered, self-assured, unshakened, and un-fazed person in you because one of the main things holding you back that you fail to admit is people. What people will think about you. What people will say about you. How people will talk about you. People. The opinions of people is one of the greatest challenges to overcome as someone who has a burning purpose deep down on the inside of them. I believe the reason this is is because we don't realize how much of our lives we spend trying to please or impress people.

For example, My mom used to swear that we wore noth-ing but name brand clothing in elementary school. I rarely remember wearing name brand clothing, but according to her, we used to rock all the nicest things. Yeah right, *eye roll* lol. Anyhow, if you grew up in the type of culture that I grew up in, then you know that the first day of school was EVERY-THING. Why was this the case? It wasn't to meet the teachers, it wasn't because you were excited to see all of your friends that you missed over the summer, and it wasn't even to feast your eyes on last year's crush. You couldn't sleep the night before the first day because you couldn't wait to show every-body your "first day" outfit. Yep, that's right. Your first day's outfit was like a ritual. You would make sure it was ironed the night before. You would lay it out on your bed and stay up throughout the night with anticipation because you couldn't wait for everyone to see it.

I remember my first day outfit in elementary school like it was yesterday. I had gotten some brand new FILAS. I just knew I was about to kill it. I had my nicely pressed white t-shirt with my blue jean Levi 501's and my fresh pair of FILAS. You couldn't tell me anything. The world was my oyster. I could not be stopped. I remember strutting down the hallway...head up, chest out, speaking to other kids who I really didn't even know. Anyone who looked at me could tell I was feeling my-self. As I was strutting down the hall, a boy stopped me and I could tell he was looking at my shoes. I mean, it was pretty obvious because he was pointing at them. In my head, I said to myself,"I know you like these, these are fresh, aren't they?" As I got closer, I started to realize how wrong I was. He wasn't amazed at my shoes. He was laughing at them. He must have talked about me for 2 of the longest minutes of my life be-cause I was wearing FILAS. I felt low. My posture changed. My chest deflated and my head had fallen. He took all the wind out of my sails.

I can tell you from that day forward I never wore those shoes again. Here's the crazy part about that as I think back on it now. I actually liked those shoes. But I never wore them again because somebody else didn't like them. I start with this story because for the most part, we spend most of our lives avoiding doing things that we actually enjoy because we're afraid of what people will think about us. In hip hop culture, there's this bravado that hip hop artists live their lives not caring what anybody thinks about them. But this is far from the truth. If they didn't care what people thought about them, why wear the fancy jewelry? Why drive the most expensive cars? Why brag about your belongings in your songs? It's because they care deeply about what people think about them. All of the expensive things that they've acquired are to impress people. The thing is, like that boy in middle school who talked about my FILAS, even if people were impressed, what you achieve will never impress everyone.

Do you know how exhausting it is to live your life for the applause of people? Not only is it exhausting, it's unsustainable.

Do you know how exhausting it is to live your life for the applause of people? Not only is it exhausting, it's unsustainable.

If you spent the majority of your life trying to make people happy, you would only self-destruct. There is no possible way that you could please everyone. There is no possible way that you could meet everyone's expectations. You will eventually let them down. You will eventually fail them, and fall short of their confidence. So why even try if you know this to be true? Look, I'm not saying that you shouldn't care what anybody thinks of you because that is completely unreasonable. If you didn't care what anybody thought of you, it wouldn't matter how you dressed when you went to work. As long as you do your job correctly it shouldn't matter how you dress right? Yeah right. We know that this is not the case. It shouldn't matter how you show up in court after you've gotten a speeding ticket right? But how you present yourself could be the difference between a judge being lenient and letting you take a defensive driving course, or you having to pay your $500 fine in full. How you present yourself matters. Everyone should care what people think about them at some level or another. But when you let their thoughts control who you become and stop you from walking in your purpose, you've crossed a dangerous line.

Everyone should care what people think about them at some level or another. But when you let their thoughts control who you become and stop you from walking in your purpose, you've crossed a dangerous line.

Let me tell you how much we as people care what others think of us. Have you ever been out somewhere and you were truly enjoying yourself? Maybe you were trying a new restaurant and you wanted to share your experience with your family and friends on social media. You take about 20 pictures of your plate of food, and you try to find someone who doesn't mind taking a picture of you in front of the restaurant. You took about twenty of those as well. Then you spend maybe 30 minutes trying to write the caption to your picture. Finally, after you've gotten everything just the way you want it, you've chosen the right filter, and everything looks great. You decide to post this picture to your social media account. You really enjoyed where you went, and deep down, you're hoping the people that see your post like it as well. After posting your photo, you wait about an hour to check and see if your picture has received any responses. To your surprise, only four people liked your post.

This is when you start to psycho-anaylyze what happened. Eventually, because this post didn't get as much attention that you hoped, you decide to take it down. Have you ever done this before? I have. The sad reality is that you weren't posting it solely because you just wanted people to be a part of this amazing experience you had at this restaurant. No, you posted it because you wanted to impress someone. You wanted your picture to get some type of response. The sad reality is just sharing a nice experience you had wasn't enough for you; you were looking for, even needed, their affirmation. You needed them to like it as much as you liked it. And because they didn't, you took it down. So really you weren't posting it for yourself, you were posting it for them.

How many times throughout your life have you stopped doing something that you were really proud of because of how someone on the outside responded to it? I stopped wearing my FILAS even though I liked those shoes. Many times throughout our life, we've done the same thing. Most people spend most of their lives second guessing themselves because every one of their actions doesn't come with the approval of people they care about. Their disapproval will often speak louder and make you shrink into a corner second guessing yourself. Just like removing a post from social media, we've removed ourselves from so many life changing situations because someone along the way didn't approve of our decision.

The post didn't get many likes so you took it down. I wonder, figuratively speaking of course, how many times in your life have you taken posts down because people didn't like it. You're going to college to be a teacher, and someone you admire told you, "Why go to college to be a teacher? Educators don't make enough money. You need to be an engineer." Though you love the fact that through teaching you get to possibly change hundreds of lives, that small comment planted a seed of doubt. That seed of doubt would eventually grow into a deeply rooted tree that will have you comparing yourself to people's opinions of what you should do for years to come.

That seed of doubt would eventually grow
into a deeply rooted tree that will have you

comparing yourself to people's opinions of what you should do for years to come.

But why? Why do we spend our time comparing ourselves to other people? I mean, shouldn't we already know that every individual is different? Look around. Can you find anybody who looks identical to you? Maybe if you're an identical twin you could find someone who has the exact same features of you, but that's rare. And even if you were an identical twin, twins are not a carbon copy of one another. They have things about them that make them unique. Why is it so hard for us to embrace what makes each and every one of us different? It was said by Jake Humphrey on Twitter, that scientists say the odds of you being born are at least 1 in 400 trillion, maybe even 1 in 400 quadrillion. That is incredibly unlikely to the point of impossible. But yet here you are, a human being with flesh and blood. Just the fact that you're walking on the face of this earth as a human being means that you are a literal miracle.

Yet, we spend most of our lives wishing we were someone else. Isn't that wild when you think about it? How crazy is it that you've been given this extremely unlikely opportunity of being born a human, and you spend the majority of your life comparing yourself to somebody else's highlight reel? Why is that?

Well, I want you to know first that comparison is a normal part of the human experience. I don't want to present the concept of comparison like it's all bad.

Well, I want you to know first that comparison is a normal part of the human experience. I don't want to present the concept of comparison like it's all bad. That's what most experts do in this space. But the reality is, some comparison is healthy and normal for development. People constantly evaluate themselves and others, in domains like attractiveness, wealth, intelligence, and success. According to some studies, as much as 10 percent of our thoughts involve comparisons of some kind. Social Comparison Theory is the idea that individuals determine their own social and personal worth based on how they stack up against others. This may sound bad at face value because of what we've been molded to believe in this current westernized culture, but let's dig a little deeper.

Let's say that I have a mentor who's had a successful 30-year marriage. I aspire to have a marriage that reflects the longevity of his marriage. As a single man, I might compare myself to him and see where I can make improvements in my life to develop the characteristic traits that I need to develop a 30-year marriage myself. Another example - My friend might have a successful career as a program manager. I'm a program manager as well, but my career has taken off like his has. Of course, I compare my career to his and try to see where I went wrong. I might ask myself questions like, "Why is he getting job offers from all the top companies but I'm not?" "How is it that we've been in the same field for the same length of time, he's elevated and moved up but I'm still stuck in the same position?" You may have a friend who has the same number of kids as you. Your friend's kids are polite and respectful. But your kids are unruly and misbehave. The friend with the kids who misbehaves might look at her friend's kids and ask herself,"How does she get her kids to be so cooperative?" These are all comparisons, and whether we want to or not, we all do it. These kinds of questions are natural for human beings to ask because we all want to evolve and elevate.

The problem with these types of questions is when we let our egos drag us into a mental game of unhealthy competition. The reason that I'm able to approach my friend and say, "Hey, I see that you have some of the biggest firms competing in a bidding war to hire you. I'm in the same field that you're in but I have not had that level of success. Can you show me what you did because obviously, I'm doing something wrong"...is because there's no ego involved for me. I'm not trying to take his place, nor am I envious or jealous of him; therefore I can move in humility, knowing that this friend might have the keys to my next level. And I'm not too prideful to admit that.

The difference between unhealthy and healthy comparison is what your comparison makes you do, and how your comparison makes you feel after you're done comparing.

The difference between unhealthy and healthy comparison is what your comparison makes you do, and how your comparison makes you feel after you're done comparing. If I compare myself to someone who has 1 million followers on Instagram and it makes me develop a plan to put out content - I see how frequently they post, I look at their posting style, and do my research to learn what would be the best practices and how they can apply to me. I tell myself that I'd like to have a million followers like they do and then put a plan together to get there, and I also execute on the plan. There's nothing wrong with that because me comparing myself to that person has actually motivated me. They've provoked me to action. I would say that the results of my comparison were healthy.

So you see, all comparisons aren't bad. Social comparison can be highly beneficial when people use social networks to push themselves. In a study, friendly competition was highly effective in pushing people to exercise more, as peers pushed each other to keep up and do more. Comparisons are a normal part of human cognition and can be good for the self-improvement process. When we compare ourselves to others, we get information about what we want and where we want to be, and we get valuable feedback on how we measure up. However, they can also cause us a lot of psychological pain.

Now conversely, if I follow this person who has 1 million followers and looking at their growth has only made me feel worse about myself; it's only made me more critical of my life, made me question my existence and purpose in an unhealthy manner, made me develop envy, jealousy, and resentment, or it's made me depressed and unmotivated like I'm not good enough. These feelings won't lead to healthy results. They will only lead to anxiety, stress, depression or worse. This is when comparison becomes destructive.

Did you know that Theodore Roosevelt called comparison "The thief of joy,"? Though sometimes comparison can be beneficial to social improvement, it can also be devastating for our mental health. Why? It can promote judgmental, biased, and overly competitive or superior attitudes. So be mindful of both sides, and also be aware that everyone has completely different life experiences. Your path is your own. Don't fall prey to the trap of comparison.

How do you overcome comparison?

STEP 1. Don't Follow Their Path, Follow Their Principles

I need you to understand something, and hopefully this frees you from the chains of unhealthy comparison. EVERY-ONE'S PATH IS DIFFERENT. Just because something worked for someone else doesn't mean that exact path is going to work for you. Don't waste valuable time comparing yourself to other people because everyone's path is distinctive. If you try to follow their path, you'll find yourself slipping into un-healthy comparisons because their path is for them, and your path is for you. Instead of following their path, follow their principles. Principles are universal. Principles are core values that can be applied to any path. If you work hard, if you stay consistent, if you are patient, if you're an adaptive learner, and if you find a mentor that's aligned with your purpose, then good things will likely happen. Why? Because those are founding principles that can be applied to any path. Follow their principles, but forge your path.

Follow their principles, but forge your path.

When I first started my business, I used to deal with "shiny object syndrome". One of the reasons why this is is because I lacked patience. But also because I was trying to do what I saw other successful entrepreneurs do. I was young. And you know when you're young, you're optimistic. You're hopeful. You're hungry. But, you're also impressionable. I wasn't thinking about my "path". I wasn't considering my "purpose". I just wanted to be successful, and what happened was I wasted a good portion of my entrepreneurial journey trying to follow other people's path. Now don't get me wrong, I learned a lot and I'm not sure I'd be where I am right now without the process I went through. But at the same time, I wish someone had told me, "Take the principles but forge your own path."

Have a potent marketing strategy that speaks to the pain points of your customers and helps them solve their problem. That's a principle. Have a sales strategy that helps you diagnose your prospects' problems, and then build trust and confidence in them that you can help them solve it. That's a principle. It doesn't matter what industry you're in, that principle applies universally. I didn't understand this at the beginning of my entrepreneurial journey.

I don't care what anyone tells you; if you don't love what you do, you won't do it for long, or you'll experience significant mental health problems if you continue doing what you don't have love for.

Therefore, I tried to do what they did, and guess what happened? Some of it didn't work, some of it did. I learned a lot, made thousands of dollars, but I was still unhappy. And I don't care what anyone tells you; if you don't love what you do, you won't do it for long, or you'll experience significant mental health problems if you continue doing what you don't have love for. I loved being an entrepreneur, but my company still felt like a job that I had to drag myself into. I became an entrepreneur because I wanted to chart a path for myself. I didn't want anyone telling me when I should work and when I could take a vacation. I wanted to build something that I could leave for my kids, and kids' kids when I passed on. I wanted to leave something that both of my fathers never left me when they passed away, a financial inheritance. I wanted to do something that would change the next generation, something that would shake the media and entertainment industry for centuries to come. It wasn't just the money that I was in it for. I was in it for legacy.

So how did I end up finding myself on the hamster wheel of unhappiness, even though I'd become a full time entrepreneur? It was because I compared my journey of entrepreneurship to someone else's journey and ended up getting trapped on their path. They had success in this area so surely I can, right? So I decided that I was just going to do what they did and surely it'll work for me, right? Wrong and right. Yes, I made money, but unfortunately, it still left me empty like that. I'd invested thousands of dollars into programs and coaching and if I'm honest, one of them worked. I started doing what my coach had instructed me to do but found myself completely unfulfilled. But the principles he shared with me were life changing for my business. I acquired skills that could translate in any industry. Since I didn't really have a blueprint for what starting a mission centered business that makes money looks like, I had to set out to figure it out on my own, and that's what I did. After learning the principles, it was time for me to chart my own path.

I can't sit here and lie and tell you that there still weren't a lot of mental roadblocks that I had to overcome to find my way. But learning these skills and the principles helped tremendously along the way. I had to clear my head of voices that would cloud my judgment. When you're so busy watching everyone else's highlight reel you inevitably start to mimic their movements. You start to imitate their behaviors. Have you ever hung around a person for so long that you started to talk like them? You started to walk like them. You started to use language that they would use. It wasn't that you were intentionally trying to copy their swag. It just happened because you've spent so much time around them that you unintentionally started to pick up on their style. This is what it was like at the beginning of my entrepreneurial journey. I was so busy spending my time following other successful leaders, experts, and entrepreneurs that I began to follow their path as if I didn't have my own. The reality is, I lost myself. I lost my mission. I lost it trying to be like people that I looked up to. I chose their path over my own.

STEP 2: Having A Deep Sense of Gratitude

Look, you may not be where you want to be but you surely aren't where you used to be. One of the pitfalls of unhealthy comparison is it robs you of your gratitude. How can you be grateful for what you have if you're constantly comparing your achievements, or lack thereof to somebody else's? The secret to a life where you're not caught in the claws of comparison is a life filled with thankfulness. In my home where we grew up, it was customary for the family to come together for dinner and pray over our food. I'll admit, prayer used to be annoying, especially when you were hungry. But in that moment of prayer, though I wasn't really paying attention at the time because I couldn't escape the growl of my stomach, I knew that it was a moment where we came together and simply thanked God for what we have. We didn't have a big house. We often had to share our room with guests. I had to wear friends' clothes to school. We barely had any money and we never took a family vacation. But we did have family. We had us, and we had this meal.

Sometimes, you can become so familiar with what you have that you take it for granted. Though I hated when it was my week to clean the kitchen because we had a big family, just the fact that we had a kitchen to clean is something to be grateful for. To have food to cook in our pots so that we could fill our bellies was something to be grateful for. We may not have had prime steak but honestly, as kids we didn't know that, because we didn't care. To us, it was fine dining.

Let me ask you, how many times have you heard of someone getting into a relationship and everything going so well at the beginning? This person was so nice and accommodating. They went the extra mile, they were kind, they were thoughtful. And then overtime, they changed. They didn't drastically change into someone else, like they were putting on a performance from the beginning and act 1 had now come to a close. No. They just don't do the things that they used to do. They became too familiar with the person that they were dating.

When this happens, people start to overlook the qualities that they found so fascinating about this individual, qualities that they found attractive. They tend to start to overlook those qualities and hone in on the things that they're starting not to like. This is where the resentment starts, and sometimes resentment, when like a snowball down a hill, is out of control, love becomes unrepairable. You wish they were the person you fell head over heels for when you all first met. But that was only a part of who they are. As you two grew closer, like an onion, the layers started to peel away. You started noticing that these layers revealed some unpleasantries, and now you're second guessing if you even want to be with them. You are starting to become dissatisfied.

In these moments of dissatisfaction, most people retreat out of fear of getting their heart broken. They develop defense mechanisms that help them protect themselves from future heart ache. But I wonder. What if during those moments you only focused on what you truly enjoyed about this person. I wonder what would happen if you ONLY thought about how grateful you are to have them in your life. Do you truly understand how any relationship could be salvaged if both individuals had a deep level of gratitude towards each other? Love would be unstoppable.

Do you truly understand how any relationship could be salvaged if both individuals had a deep level of gratitude towards each other? Love would be unstoppable.

But we all know that this isn't the case. Usually resentment builds. You take each other for granted, and then the relationship ends. That's what happens when you don't have gratitude. A lack of gratitude is like a little cancer. It goes undetected at the beginning, but over time as it builds, it starts to kill all of your vital organs until it's too late to repair. Dissatisfaction would never allow you to see the beauty of your situation, because if you did, gratitude would no longer let you live your life as a victim. You would appreciate every part of your journey.

Unhealthy comparison makes you position yourself as the victim in every situation. Victims are never in control of their life or situation.

Unhealthy comparison makes you position yourself as the victim in every situation. Victims are never in control of their life or situation. They blame everyone else for their circumstances. When you compare yourself to others, it makes you feel worthless and demoralized, unable to get what you want and "deserve," and you resent others for what they have. You see how the latter statement positions you to be the victim? Life happens to you instead of you happening to life. When you see yourself as the victim, you can't really appreciate the opportunities afforded to you. You can't see the beauty in those opportunities.

You want to know something? The only reason I really cared about what other people were wearing was because I was comparing myself to everyone else. In actuality, the clothes were fine. I liked them. I only started not to like them when I started to notice what other people were wearing. That's the toxic nature of comparison. You can actually enjoy your life. You can enjoy your job, family, and relationship status,hat is, until you start to look at everyone else and compare their lives to yours. Who's more happy, the multi-millionaire who lives in the loft and can buy anything, or the girl who lives a modest life on a farm with her family? Happiness is relative. The multi-millionaire can be just as happy as the girl raised on a farm. But you know what would strip both individuals of their happiness? If they started to compare themselves to each other. If the farm girl said,"My life sucks, look at all of the nice things the millionaire can buy, and I can only afford to go to my local market and buy my favorite bag of chips..."; or if the millionaire said,"I wish my life was as simple as the farm girl. Everyone wants something from me, and I feel like no one genuinely loves me...". You fall into the trap of comparing yourself, and you will never feel like what you have or what you've achieved is good enough.

Don't let comparison rob you of your happiness, because happiness is a choice. You can choose to be happy. It'll just be hard to see the beauty through the ashes if you're too busy looking at everyone else.

HAVE PATIENCE IN YOUR PERSISTENCE

One of the best, yet most frustrating things I've ever been told is that it's not time yet. "Joshua, I know you feel like you're ready right now but, you have to wait." "Anything worth having is worth waiting for." As a child, hearing something like this, I felt it was baloney. Do you remember a time as a kid, you might have asked for something you really wanted right then in that moment, but you had to wait? And then you had the audacity to ask your mom or dad, "Why?" "Why can't I have it now?" "Why do I have to wait?" You would throw a fit. Your posture would change. You would pout all because you couldn't get what you wanted at that moment. We've all been there. Growing up in a Black home when they told you "No", oftentimes, they didn't even give an explanation. It was just "NO". It was so frustrating because if you're going to tell me "No", at least tell me why I can't have what I want right now.

But that often wasn't the case. I just had to accept that I may never know why they said, "No".

Manytimes, life will tell us, "No". We get upset. We quit. We pout. We take it as a sign that maybe we're going in the wrong direction because it seems like we're getting told "no" at every turn. But here's what I need you to know. Oftentimes, "No" is just a shorter version for "not right now". That's why you have to have patience in your persistence.

I remember I used to be a part of a Christian rap group called Still Trill Christians. We experienced a lot of success in our time as Christian rappers, and were the first Christian rap group to be featured on a major television network, BET. We were the first Christian rap group to ever be featured on a world wide, number 1 rated, talk show, and the first and only Christian rap group to be awarded by a sitting President, former President Barack Obama for our song called "No Sex". Yep, all of this success that we experienced was centered around a song about abstinence, lol. It's actually funny when I think about it. God has a great sense of humor.

Anyhow, the reason I needed to give you the history was because at that time, we were very popular,especially within our city, Houston. We had a lot of younger aspiring Christian rappers who wanted to do what we were doing. Of course, anyone would be attracted to the fame and notoriety we were receiving. Fame can be a blessing, but it can also be a curse if you don't know how to deal with it. There are a lot of famous, unhappy, depressed people. I appreciated that so many younger guys wanted us to mentor them. But most of them were in it for the fame and prestige that we had received. We were in it for the mission. We didn't allow the fame to go to our heads because we had mentors, and our mentors kept us grounded.

So, when the young guys expressed interest in wanting to be a part of our movement, we welcomed them with open arms. But we also expressed to them that they would have to be mentored before they were ready to perform on stages. See, when you're on that stage and you hear people screaming your name, crying, and becoming extremely emotional at the mere fact of your presence, it can go to your head. It's very intoxicating. If you're not careful, you will be overcome by it. You will forget the mission and start to do it for the applause, the validation, and or the approval of people. We didn't want our mentees to fall into that trap, so we put them on a mentor track before we would allow them to perform on live stages.

I remember one of our mentees at the time had come to me frustrated because he felt he was ready to start performing. I knew deep down inside that he wasn't ready because he had some destructive character flaws. He was too eager to be on the stage. For us, the stage was just a place that we could minister to people. But for him I could tell that the stage was just another place to show people how talented of a rapper he was. He was good. Really good. The problem with that is, just because you're good doesn't mean you're ready. So when he kept coming to me, practically begging to let him rap, I finally told him one day, "YOU NOT READY YET".

I didn't give him an explanation as to why I felt he wasn't ready yet, I just told him he wasn't ready yet. Looking back on this in retrospect, if I had known what I know now, keeping in mind I was 21-22 at the time, I would have told him why I didn't think he was ready yet. We were rapping not because we wanted fame or fancy cars, but because we wanted to share our message with a generation who desperately needed it. I would have told him his hunger for the stage and the praise of people will eventually have him self-destruct. People will praise with their lips one moment and then curse you with those same lips the next. I didn't go into all of this detail when I told him he wasn't ready yet. As a young man myself, I didn't quite know how to articulate that. But I knew the reservation I had about allowing him to grace the stage was real. I didn't want the stage and lights to cause him to implode.

Can you guess what his response was to me telling him that "You're not ready yet?" He got really angry. He felt that I was hating and trying to hold him back. He felt like I was threatened by his gift to rap and I didn't want to see him win. That of course was far from the truth. He tried to stick around but I knew that he would eventually leave if he kept the same mentality. How could you be mentored by someone that you felt was "hating" on you? Eventually, he stopped coming to shows, stopped coming to meetings, and branched off on his own...all because he felt like "he was ready". Needlesstosay, unfortunately his rap career never quite panned out.

See, you may be thinking that you're ready. You may feel like you're ready. You might even be really gifted in the areas of your pursuits. But feeling like you're ready isn't a real indicator that you are. So when you're being told "No", it's often a sign that you're not ready. There's still development that needs to happen in you to prepare you for the level that you're going to. So instead of being jaded, sad, disheartened and discouraged, take rejection as a "not right now", not as a hard "No".

I wish my mentee at the time would have taken my "No" as "not right now". I wasn't telling him that we'd NEVER allow him to grace the stage, or we'd never allow him to show the world what he could do. Me telling him no was my attempt to prevent him from being overcome by his ambition. He needed patience, the virtue of patience - the ability to wait for something without getting angry or upset. Just the mere fact of him getting upset verified to me that he wasn't ready. If he would have been a little more patient, he would have been recommended to every opportunity we were not able to fulfill on. He would have been introduced to every resource we had, and exposed to our connections and network. But what he had was ambition, and ambition without patience is disastrous.

Sometimes, it isn't your skills or gifts that take you to the next level, sometimes it's an endorsement.

My mentee at the time didn't understand just how powerful it was to be associated with someone powerful. He was too young to truly grasp the concept of an endorsement. Sometimes, it isn't your skills or gifts that take you to the next level, sometimes it's an endorsement. Sometimes you have to be number 4 before you can be number 1. But being number 4 isn't a bad thing, especially if being number 4 gets you in the room. So many people desire to be number 1, when in actuality, they're not ready for the responsibility that comes with being number 1. The benefit of being mentored by somebody who is number 1, 2, or 3, is that you get a chance to observe and learn from their mistakes without making them yourself. You can quietly be observing the room, and though none of the powerful people care who you are at the time, trust me, they notice you. Unfortunately, my mentee's ego moved him out of position. He wasn't now. But HE WAS NEXT.

Sometimes you have to be number 4 before you can be number 1. But being number 4 isn't a bad thing, especially if being number 4 gets you in the room.

That's the thing about ego. Ego will try to convince you that you're better than you actually are. And when you find out that you're not as good as you thought, you take a hit to your pride. This is because you lack humility. There was something missing that you needed in order to take advantage of the opportunity. Instead of being negatively critical of yourself, take that as an opportunity to learn and develop. Guess what, you missed the mark, and that's OK. There's no need to get angry or feel embarrassed about it. You just weren't ready yet.

A lack of patience will trick you into moving before your time.

A lack of patience will trick you into moving before your time. Let me say that again, a lack of patience will TRICK YOU into moving BEFORE YOUR TIME. You may think you're ready, but the reality is that you are not. If you were, you would already be where you desired to be. But, you're not there yet. Instead of being discontent, and instead of being discontent once you've come to this truth, realize that even though you aren't where you want to be, if you persist, you will get there.

My mom used to love telling us, "No". At times, I felt as though this was her favorite word. I mean, before we could even get the question out of our mouth, the answer was always "No". Like dang, can I at least ask the question first, lol. I remember asking my mom about an allowance, "Can we be compensated for washing the dishes and cleaning the kitchen weekly." Her response was, "You're already being paid." I was confused because I did not remember one time she'd put any cash in my hands. I was like "Mama, you've never paid us for cleaning the kitchen." She responded, "Yes, I have." I sat there confused, because I know that if she'd given us money for cleaning the kitchen, I would remember that. She laughed as she looked at how confused I was. Then she proceeded to respond, "Do you feel that cool a/c blowing? Look up, do you see that nice roof over your head? And do you remember who cooked that meal that you just ate? How did the food get there? It surely didn't just appear out of nowhere! You are being paid because I pay for everything in this house...now go on somewhere and leave me alone." I was salty as I walked away.

She had a valid point, it still didn't make me feel any better though. Appreciating the roof over my head wasn't the same as being paid money in hand. This conversation frustrated me. Keep in mind, we had a BIG family. On top of that, my parents were ministers who believed in opening their doors to people in need. So, not only was it the 6 of us in the immediate family, I don't remember our house being just 6 of us at all. I think there were at least 9 people staying in that house at any given time. So, you can imagine how many dishes we had to wash. I felt like I was on dish duty at a restaurant after dinner. It was dreadful.

Nevertheless, my disappointed demeanor wouldn't change my mother's mind. I had to figure out another way to put some money in my pockets. Since my parents wouldn't pay me for washing dishes, I had to figure something else out. This is when I learned how to create a flyer in Word Art, printed it out, and walked around the neighborhood asking people if they'd let me cut their yard and wash their car for $25 bucks. When I think about it now, I'm like, "Man they were getting a steal!" Lol. My mom's denial actually opened up another opportunity for me that I don't know if I would have been introduced to, had she not told me "No". There's always great potential in "No". It's your choice to look at the glass half empty or the glass half full. But if you see the opportunity in the midst of

"No", you'll find out that a "No" is just a delayed "Yes". You just have to be persistent.

I started mowing yards and washing cars that summer. I was able to go to the corner store and buy all the chips and candy I wanted. One day, my mom asked me, "Where are you getting the money to buy all of these things?" I told her I'd started cutting grass and washing cars. She smiled. "My son is a go-getter. I'm proud of you." After saying that, she took a $20 dollar bill out of her purse and gave it to me. She said, "Keep being great, you deserve this. And guess what? You don't have to wash dishes this week." I was overjoyed! Not only did I get paid, I didn't have to wash dishes to get the money. She just gave it to me because she was proud of me. A delayed "No", that eventually led to a "Yes".

We look at the word "No" as denial when it's really temporary delayed approval.

The reason most of us have problems with getting told "No" is because we don't understand that "No" is only momentary. Someone will say "Yes" you just have to adapt, persist, and then ask again. We look at the word "No" as denial when it's really temporary delayed approval. This is why we need patience. Patience allows you to persist through denial. Have you ever heard the story of the rabbit and the turtle? The rabbit was faster but the turtle won the race because he persisted and went at his own pace.

I want to tell you a funny story. When I was 18, I told myself that I would be rich at the age of 26. You couldn't convince me of anything different. I knew it would happen. Then, my 26th birthday came and I was far from rich, not even close. When I was a part of this christian rap group, we were offered a 3 million dollar record label deal. The deal had one contingency - we had to remove the word "christian" from our name. We were young and zealous at the time, and there was no way we would do such a thing. But I can't lie and say that I didn't think about it. If we would have signed that deal, I would have accomplished my goal of being rich by 26. I was 23 at the time with a 3 million dollar record deal on the table. You want to know the first thing I thought about buying once we closed our deal? An orange lamborghini. I wanted to show everyone that I had made it. All the doubters and naysayers, take that!

Remember when I told you about my mentee? He was too immature to stick around because of his ambition. Well, I was too immature to understand what to do with 3 million dollars. Had I signed that deal, never being exposed to that amount of money a day in my life, I would have blown through it. Also, I didn't take into consideration that 3 million had to be split among 5 of us, and 20% for the manager. That would leave us with having to equally split $2,400,000 among 4 of us which equates to each one of us getting $600,000 a piece. Then there are taxes - the tax rate is about 30%, which would have left me with $422,000, if I was smart enough to actually pay my taxes. My Lamborghini would have cost me $150,000 because

I would have had to pay for it in cash...I need to make a statement. Then, there's buying a home, buying my mom a car, and etc etc etc. I didn't have mentors who knew how to point me in the right direction. On top of that, the 3 million dollars they offered us was actually an advance, which means that it was just a loan from the record companies. We would have had to pay all of that back before seeing any money from our record deal. I didn't know any of this at the time. Had we taken that deal, we might be still paying that back to this day if we didn't have a smash hit.

To say the least, I didn't understand what it meant to sign a record deal at that level. I would have blown through that money quickly because I wasn't ready yet. I wasn't mature enough to handle that kind of money at 23-years old. I was ill-equipped. When I look back on that record deal knowing what I know now, I ask myself, "Joshua, would you have signed that deal back then knowing what you know now?" Of course I would have, if I knew what I know now. I would have gotten a lawyer that I could trust, gotten a group of financial advisors, and started planning future investments. I would not have bought a lamborghini. I would have paid cash for a nice low grade Mercedes, paid off some debt, and put the rest back into investments and savings. I don't regret not taking the deal, because the truth is it probably could have destroyed me.

I'd like to think that at that time we had just enough patience to not accept the deal. We weren't really sure what would've happened had we accepted the deal, but one thing we knew for sure is that we didn't want to compromise our values. If we had compromised our values for money, what would that say about us? If we compromised on something like signing a deal that made us compromise our conscience, what other areas in our life would we have eventually made compromises on? Though 3 million seemed like the no brainer option, this was only a quick fix to problems our character wasn't ready for. Truth is, I wasn't ready to handle $600,000 dollars.

I really wish you'd sit with that statement and think about times in your life where things didn't quite go the way you liked. Ask yourself, were you REALLY ready? It's easy to feel like you're ready at the moment. You're consumed with excitement and euphoria. But if you looked back on a time where a huge opportunity passed you up, were you REALLY ready for it? I believe that the true key to lasting success is patience coupled with persistence. Persistence means that you continue to do the task until you get results, regardless of resistance you may come against. You persist. You don't give up and you refine over time as you hone your skills. The definition of persistence means to continue firmly or obstinately in a course of action in spite of difficulty or opposition. People hate the feeling of rejection when they are told "No". But what I need you to do is look at "No" as a necessary part of the process. Being told "No" is a privilege, because if you can stay the course in the midst of opposition, you're going to conquer any goal you set your mind to. There's no such thing as being persistent without difficulty or opposition.

Persistence also means to continue to endure over a prolonged period. I think that one of my qualities is the fact that I don't quit, I just outlast the competition. Sometimes, I'm not more talented. Sometimes, I'm not more gifted. Sometimes

I've only pretended to know what I was doing even though I knew I didn't have a clue, and sometimes, they are better, faster, and stronger. But I don't approach life like it's a sprint, I approach life like a marathon. You expend a great amount of energy running sprints. You may even get first place, in the short-term. But after a sprint is finished the race is done. People like to do life in sprints when really it's a marathon.

I remember one time I was at my local gym, and one of the activities that I really like to do for cardio is to go swimming in the lap pool. There was this older Hispanic guy who was swimming in the lane next to me. Of course, because I'm competitive, I entered into a competition with him in my head. He was already swimming when I got in the pool. I wanted to catch him. He was like maybe a lap ahead of me. If you know me, then you know I'm a very fast swimmer, so off I went. I'm swimming as fast as I possibly can and eventually I shortened the distance between us, but there was a problem. I could not keep up that pace so I had to take long breaks to catch my breath. But this guy, he NEVER stopped swimming. I kid you not.

I thought he would be like me and have to catch his breath eventually as well, but he didn't. He kept the same pace the entire time and never stopped swimming. So, after I caught my breath, I took off again and shortly after, I stopped again to catch my breath. This vicious cycle happened over and over and over again. FINALLY, I barely caught up with him, but I had to stop because I was winded. And again, he kept on swimming. Ultimately, I eventually gave up because every time I put forth a burst of energy to swim my fastest, the more tired

I became. And I saw the distance between him and I become greater and greater. He won the race that day that he didn't even know he was in lol.

Why is this important? I want you to know that the man's technique wasn't better than mine. I was actually the better, faster swimmer. But he had something that I lacked: he knew how to control his breathing and pace himself. All I wanted to do was win just to say that I won. It would stroke my ego and make me feel accomplished. But he wasn't in a race with me. I was in a race with him while he was running his own race. I couldn't keep up with his pace and therefore I lost.

I was in a race with him while he was running his own race. I couldn't keep up with his pace and therefore I lost.

The point is, he outlasted me. He also humbled me. No matter how fast I thought I was, that day, he was unbeatable because speed didn't matter. He was playing the long game. I was you to think of life in this way. Think of it as a marathon. You're playing the long game and if you take time to smell the roses, you can learn a lot throughout the process. You can't approach life and your purpose like a sprint. If you're so busy trying to get to the finish line you'll miss a lot of the lessons along the way. You need to be just as in love with the process as you are with the prize. This takes patience and persistence.

*You need to be just as in love with the
process as you are with the prize.*

Quick wins can be detrimental to your growth in the grand scheme of things. A lot of times we experience quick wins in our lives but we don't ask ourselves, at what cost? What did we have to sacrifice to get that quick win? Who did you have to become? What did you have to give up? Did you know that the average millionaire is 57-years old. As of 2013, 42% of millionaires are baby boomers (between 57 and 75 years of age), the majority of any age group. If becoming a millionaire was so easy, don't you think that millionaires would accomplish this feat at a much younger age? Why has it taken so long? Why don't most people become millionaires in their 20's, 30's, or even 40's? I'll tell you why. Most likely their life experience, knowledge, and skills had to catch up with their vision and ambition. Vision and ambition usually come before reaping the financial benefits of your sacrifice.

See, this entire time you probably thought you were behind, but really, you are right where you're supposed to be. You just need to be patient and embrace the process. The last thing you should do is allow your appetite to force you to your finish line before your time. I want you to ask yourself, "What is it that you could be learning right now at this point in your journey?" Sometimes, we can be so focused on the future, that we can't embrace the beauty of the present. Don't worry, if you persist, and if you're patient, you will get there. But until you get "there", what can you learn "here"? That's the question that most people should be asking themselves.

I'll admit. I used to be consumed with the future. And sometimes, your vision of the future will discourage you in your present. That's because of the timeline and expectations you put on yourself. It's funny because we think that we have that much control over our life, but the truth is we don't. We think that we can actually plan our life to a tee and it will happen in the time span that we made up for ourselves. Next thing you know, you're 30 with no marriage and no kids. But you thought you'd be married with kids by 26. When I was married, we said that we wanted to spend the first 2 years of our marriage enjoying each other. After the first two years, we'd have a kid. Two years came and as we started to try for a child we had fertility issues. You could not have told us that this would be the case at the beginning of our marriage. But there we were, in year five, still childless.

Life has a way of throwing wrenches in your plans, and if you're so consumed with the future, it can cause you to become disgruntled with the present. Have a vision for the future, because that vision for the future is what keeps pulling us forward. We're drawn to this vision that we have for ourselves and our family. It doesn't push us. It pulls us. It draws us. But don't become so obsessed with the vision of your future that you're not able to function in your present. You need to be present in your present as you prepare for your future too. These two things need to happen simultaneously. They need to co-exist.

You need to be present in your present as you prepare for your future too.

Being so consumed with the future will also make you lose patience in the present. It can make you experience anxiety in your present. No wonder why there's a famous person who said:

"Therefore I tell you, stop being worried or anxious (perpetually uneasy, distracted) about your life, as to what you will eat or what you will drink; nor about your body, as to what you will wear. Is life not more than food, and the body more than clothing? ... "So do not worry about tomorrow; for tomorrow will worry about itself. Each day has enough trouble of its own."

If you are wondering why you can never be satisfied with your present, maybe it's because you're too preoccupied with your future. When you're consumed with getting "there", how can you be content with being in the "here" and "now"? You remember when I told you that I made a promise to myself that I would be rich by the age of 26? I admit now that I didn't realize how hard it was to actually become rich. When I didn't reach my goal at 26, I felt like a failure. I'd put so much pressure on myself to be rich by 26, that when it didn't happen, I felt defeated.

I then made another promise to myself. I said to myself that…"I may not have hit my goal by 26, but I will surely hit my goal by 30." My 30th birthday came and I still was not rich. I kind of laugh to myself as I think about it. Guess what, I was disappointed again. I felt like a failure again. Then one day in prayer and meditation, I had a thought. That thought was…"Whenever I'm supposed to be rich it will be, and if it may never be I will be ok with that, but I won't stop trying. I will persist." Can you imagine the load taken off of me when I said this? I felt like the world was lifted off my shoulders. I realized at that moment that I was so focused on the finish line, that there was no way I could enjoy the journey.

When you're focused on the finish line, you always feel rushed. You can never live in the moment. You can never appreciate the fact that you're even in the race because it's all about how you place. "I need to get first place, second place, third place." "I need to place or else I'm a failure and shouldn't even be participating in this event called life." Again, this is pressure that you put on yourself that doesn't allow you to take it in, and appreciate the fact that you have legs. You can participate. You're still here. You have another chance. You have another shot. When you rush, you second-handedly rob yourself of joy. But when you pace yourself, you're taking in every breath, every moment. You're grateful for where you've come, even though you know you have further to go. A person like that doesn't feel anxiety or stress because they're not where they want to be, they're too grateful for how far they've come. And like the asian guy who was swimming in the next lane over, they continue to swim. They continue to just focus on their race.

In our generation, patience isn't a virtue. We feel rushed. We typically don't like to wait for anything. And can you blame us? How can anyone who has immediate access to everything be expected to wait for anything? If you asked me to identify the worst characteristic trait of this generation, I would say patience. We lack patience. We have access to everything we need in our hands because of technology. If we need a recipe for dinner, we can google it. If we don't know how to spell a word, it autocorrects our spelling immediately. If I wanted to learn how to fix a broken part on my vehicle. I can YouTube it and most likely find an instructional video solving my problem immediately. Can you really expect a generation who has access to everything at their fingertips to have patience?

That's a big ask.

Because of instant access to solutions, people, resources, and etc, I think that this has created a sense of entitlement within us. I mean, think about it. Technology is here to serve us. If we had a question we didn't know the answer to and we googled it, Google wouldn't reply, "I'm sorry, I have the answer, but I think you would benefit from going to the library and reading {insert self-help book}. If Google did that then people would stop using the platform. We're looking for answers. We need the questions to be resolved immediately. Access to the web has made us addicted to quick turnarounds and fast solutions. But what we fail to realize is that life doesn't work like that. Life ebbs and flows. There's no quick way to lose weight. You won't be able to learn how to read in 30 seconds. You won't be able to speak a new language fluently in a week's time. But technology has made us believe in the impractical. I fear that access to technology has played a huge part in creating unrealistic expectations in us on how we approach life. A result of this is that we've become extremely impatient.

When you think about it, the goal of these major tech companies is to make things faster and easier for us. The only reason this is the case is because this is what the consumer demands. The consumer demands faster, simpler, easier, solutions. We need load times on websites to be faster. We need the shipping times from our online retailers to be faster. We need the wait times while sitting in our favorite fast-food lines to be faster. We need shorter videos on social media, they need to be quick and snappy. Everything around us emboldened us with this belief system that everything we need, we can get it fast. Sure, when you're ordering something like a lamp from Amazon, you can select to get it the same day. But a lamp is far different from your purpose. You can order it and have it delivered to you the next day. There are so many factors that contribute to walking in your purpose, that's the reason why walking in your purpose takes a lifetime. You have to become a lifestudent of your purpose and that takes patience and time.

Patience is what we lack. I'll admit, I've been a victim many times of my lack of patience. I remember my old truck was having an issue. When I was slowing down, the truck would randomly cut off. You want to know the first thing I did? I went to Google and googled my problem. There were so many solutions that came up, I didn't really know where to start. A lot of the solutions were complex, so I wasn't able to fix them on my own. Since I couldn't self-diagnose the problem, I immediately got frustrated. I probably spent a couple of hours online trying to figure it out. Ask me did I solve the problem? I sure didn't. I then tried to take my car up to the local dealer, and when I pulled into the service check-in, they asked me if I had an appointment. I immediately got frustrated again..."Are you kidding me, why do I need an appointment?!" Begrudgingly, I scheduled an appointment for the next day. But who knows if my car would be operable the next day. I could only hope and pray.

So the next day, I checked in to my appointment and they told me that it would take a few days for them to run a full diagnostic on the car. They said they had a few other vehicles in front of me. My frustration is piling up. "Why would I have to schedule an appointment if you guys had a few people before me anyway?!?!" Also, I needed my car because I still needed to get around. I couldn't be without a car for a few days. "Do you guys have a loaner I can use?" I asked. "No, unfortunately all of our loaners are out." I promise you, I just could not win.

After a few days went by, they called me and told me that my car was ready. Now, anytime you take your car to the shop, you always know to expect the worst. When I checked in with my technician, I wanted them to get straight to the point. "How much is it going to cost me to fix the car?" I asked. They told me that the car basically needed a new engine and that it would take me $7,000 dollars to fix it. I laughed because there was no way I was going to pay them more money than I paid for the car to fix it. I politely told them thanks and went to get a second opinion. I took the car to a well known auto shop. They told me the issue was the grounding on the car, and that it would cost me $450 dollars to fix. I believed them and $450 sounded way cheaper than $7,000, so I let them "fix" it. After I'd gotten the car out of their shop a few days later, it started doing the same thing. They didn't fix the problem.

I took the car back to them, and am boiling at this point because I paid them and they did not fix the problem. At this point, I'm feeling like all these auto mechanics want to do is make a buck off of you. They told me they would have run another diagnostic and I said "I'm not paying for another diagnostic when I just paid you guys for a diagnostic and you didn't fix the problem." They agreed, took my car in, and ran another diagnostic. When they called me back, they told me that they had finally figured out the problem and it was going to cost me another $450 to fix. I said, "Ok, well is the car still running?" They said, "Yes." I told them that I would pick the car up and think about it. So, I went and picked up my car and guess what I did? I googled it. Could I fix this problem myself for wayyyy cheaper than $450 bucks? To my amazement, I could, and it would only cost me $25 bucks. That's right! The part was only $25 bucks and it was on the top of the engine. All I had to do was unscrew a few screws and replace the old part with the new one. It was an easy fix!

Here's my reason for telling you this story. Though the fix to my problem was easy, my route to getting to the fix was hard. It wasn't simple. It required patience. I had to go through 2 mechanic shops and waste hundreds of dollars to finally get to the fix. Why couldn't the fix be as simple to get to as it was to actually fix the car? It just wasn't. I found myself getting more and more frustrated when I had another setback. I hated the fact that I didn't immediately have a solution to my problem. But sometimes, that's how problems work. Sometimes, that's how life works. There aren't immediate solutions to the problem that we'll face.

...opposition isn't a sign that you shouldn't move forward, quite the opposite actually. Opposition is a sign that you're going in the right direction.

There are challenges that we have to overcome. There is opposition. And opposition isn't a sign that you shouldn't move forward, quite the opposite actually. Opposition is a sign that you're going in the right direction. A lot of times, people think because they're experiencing challenges, this means that they are doing something wrong. But I'm here to tell you that if you're experiencing challenges as you progress forward, you're doing something RIGHT. Don't let the challenges make you about-face and go back the way you came. No, press through the challenges until you taste victory, because victory is coming if you persist.

When I was trying to fix my car, it took me a couple months to finally figure out what the problem was. Once I finally did figure out the problem, it was only after I'd experienced opposition, and the solution cost me time and money. My solution didn't come immediately, nor did it come easily.

I want you to know that there are going to be things in your life that will happen to you that you won't be able to control. Sure, everyone wishes the route to get to their destiny would be easier, but how would we learn if we never experienced resistance? How would we grow? How would we develop? How would we get better? The path of least resistance is the path most people would like to take. Unfortunately, this path doesn't really exist. Sure, through mentorship and coaching, maybe you won't make as many mistakes as you would without it. But even if you had these things, it doesn't guarantee that your purpose is going to come easy. When you're becoming who you're born to be, you must patiently persist. This is the only way you get there.

YOU WERE BORN FOR THIS

Premise: The Hood

Though this book is about to come to its conclusion, let me start from the beginning - not the beginning of this book, but the beginning of my life. I grew up in the hood, the place where you couldn't let anyone take anything from you. If you let them slide once, they'd do it over and over and over again. They preyed on weakness in the hood. Growing up in the hood was like being constantly surrounded by sharks ready to feast on a wounded seal. They were waiting for you to start leaking blood and when you did, you were devoured. This is one of the reasons why I had such a hard time tapping into my emotions. I had a hard time expressing my feelings because there was no place for feelings as a young boy growing up in the ghetto. Feelings would get you killed.

I remember one day in elementary school there was this guy named Kyle. Everyone was afraid of Kyle. He intimated the kids. He was loud, boisterous, and had a cocky bravado. He would dare people to challenge him, and He always wanted to fight and was always in trouble. I was smaller in elementary school. Yes, even your size in the ghetto made you a target. Kyle would throw verbal jabs at me on the bus. He would do this like bump me with his shoulders and most times, I won't lie, I let him. If I'm being honest with you guys, I was afraid of Kyle too. He was a bully. He never quite took it too far with me until one day when I was waiting in line to get my breakfast. The breakfast line in the mornings at my elementary school was so long. It felt like you were waiting in line at the social security office. If you've ever been to the social security office, then you know how long the lines could be. One of the things you never let anyone do when you were waiting in line was to skip you. Skipping you in line was the ultimate sign of disrespect. If you openly let someone skip you in line and you didn't do anything about it, it would just send the message to the other sharks that you were prey. You were weak and ripe to be taken advantage of. Soon enough, you had more than one bully problem.

I gathered since Kyle never had known me to be the type of kid to stand up for myself, that he saw weakness in me. All of the times I would let his slick comments and passive aggressive behavior slide, it allowed him to build up the courage to perform the ultimate sign of disrespect: skip me in the breakfast line. So that's what he did, and he did it in front of everyone. You could hear them gasping under their breath, wondering what I was going to do. I could feel the other bullies rubbing their hands together as they watched Kyle do this without any response from me. I sat there and pondered for a minute, and the only words I could remember were the words of my dad when he told me..."Son, don't you ever let nobody punk you." Sure, I was afraid of Kyle, but I was more afraid of what my dad would think of me if I let this transgression slide without any kind of response.

So I tapped Kyle on the shoulder and said, "You ain't skipping me, you got to get to the back of the line." He turned around and laughed in my face as if I were joking. Everyone else laughed with him. I tapped him on his shoulder again, "You have to get to the back of the line, you ain't SKIPPING ME!" My tone was a little more aggravated this time than the first time around. So Kyle turned around and responded, "And if I don't, what yo b**** a** gone do about it?" This was the moment. I knew that I only had two options: back down or stand up. I knew that if I backed down right then and there, I would spend the rest of the year running from Kyle and the other sharks. I chose to stand up.

That's when I pushed him. I think he was caught off guard by my response. He didn't expect me to push him. Shoot, I didn't expect for me to push him. But I did and we got into a shoving match. We just kept pushing each other until finally, I took the first swing. It was a windmill and I was proud of my technique, but I swung, lol. We started fighting, and the entire time I was throwing wild punches with my head down. I had no clue what I was doing. Of course, the adult broke it up and dragged us to the principal's office. I could hear my peers making fun of how wild my punches were. Some even said that I "fought like a girl", but I didn't care. I took the first swing when the rest of them would probably have never swung at all. I was proud.

We moved out of the hood to the suburbs. It was funny though because the school we went to seemed like all the ghetto kids moved out of the hood to the same suburbs as well. So, it was out of the frying pan and into the fire. The environment wasn't much different. I fought a lot in high school, but my parents didn't really know about it because I never fought "at school". I was smart enough to have all of my fights outside of school. I guess that little fighter in me just grew and grew. I didn't turn into a bully because I knew how it felt to be bullied. But I sure enough didn't tolerate anyone bullying me. My mom is still surprised to this day when I tell her about all the fights that I had when we were younger.

Conclusion: The Hood Made Me

I preyed on my goals and my vision. I preyed on my purpose. I was relentless.

Even though no one wants to grow up poor, growing up in the hood can have its advantages. When you grow up around sharks, you either become a shark or you become food. I'd like to think that I became a shark. Thing is, I wasn't preying on people, I preyed on my goals and my vision. I preyed on my purpose. I was relentless. The hood made me have an edge. It made me have grit. It made me look fear in the face and say "No"! Regardless of what happens, I will not give in, I will not be afraid, and I will take up for myself and I will not let anyone push me around. I'd like to think that this played a huge role in my purpose because if you're not careful, life will push you around. Have you met that person where everything is always going bad in their life? They have no control over their circumstances, and it just seems like bad is attracted to them? I'd like to think that life is pushing this person around and they're just going with the flow. I refuse to just go with the flow of life. I want to be intentional about the choices I make, about the people I choose to hang around, and about making decisions that will set me up to receive blessings, open doors, breakthrough, and wins. I refuse to let life just man-handle me. I'm going to man-handle life, as much as I can anyway.

The hood taught me that. The hood taught me to not just sit there and take it. It taught me how to fight back. I'm glad I grew up poor, and I'm glad that I grew up in the hood. It made me look fear in the eyes and say, "No, I will not be forced into submission." It created this relentlessness in me. It taught me how to be flexible, how to think on my feet, how to observe my situation and adapt quickly, and how to make wise decisions in the midst of chaos. When you're able to be in the middle of a gang war, you have to make decisions quickly and decisively. It could literally mean life or death. The hood taught me how to bend and not break. It taught me how not to fold under pressure. It taught me that even though you're in a certain environment, you don't have to become a product of that environment, You have the power to change your circumstances.

It also taught me that if you are lazy, your environment will devour you.

...you don't have to become a product of that environment, You have the power to change your circumstances.

The hood gave me an edge. It made me have tough skin; skin that I would need to be a successful entrepreneur, skin that I would need to be able to walk into boardrooms and not feel intimidated. I literally watched people get beat to a bloody pulp with chains and bats in my front yard. There's no way I'd let some corporate executives intimidate me. The hood made me have that type of confidence. If I could survive the hood, I could surely thrive, let alone survive, an hour in meeting with a bunch of corporate executives. The hood built me "Ford Tough", and by the grace of God, I made it out. If I made it there, I could make it anywhere.

Premise: The Church

You want to know what surprised my mom even more? We were pastors' kids. Now I know what you're thinking, and I'm here to tell you that it's not true. Pastor's kids are not the worst, lol. I think people just place the same expectations on Pastors' kids that they place on their parents, without realizing that we're just kids too. Anyhow, we spent a lot of time in church. As a matter of fact, I would go so far to say that we were raised in church. We went to church at least 3 times a week, and 2-3 times on a Sunday. Church was a big part of my worldview and upbringing. Church had a big influence on who I would eventually become.

Even though my parents forced us to go to church, they never forced a relationship with God on us. They wanted us to choose that for ourselves. At the age of 19, I surrendered my life to Christ and became a Christian. One would assume that I was already a Christian because I went to church. But let me tell you, just because you go to church doesn't mean that you're a Christian. More on that in another book.

Once I became a Christian, my life got a whole lot harder. I had more responsibilities at our small church. I couldn't go out to the places that I used to go to before, and my lifestyle had to reflect one who actually practiced Christian disciplines. I had to be "different". I was never the type to "play with God". Even dudes that grew up in the streets didn't play with God. They were either in church, or they weren't. It's off that they have this saying in the hip hop community..."If you're scared, go to church." Because most of the street dudes that I know, I mean real killers, they were terrified of coming to church. It was an unspoken rule where I'm from, you just didn't play with the church or God. Anything that I put my mind to, I was 100% bought in. I wasn't going to play with God. I wanted to learn. I wanted to excel. I wanted to grow. I was sold out. My lifestyle took a 180 about face.

I remember when we were going through discipleship, we had to wake up early in the morning on Sundays and be at the church before the pastor got there. We needed to be standing in front of the church at attention, like a little army lol. Not only that, because we were leaders, we had to join the leadership on fasts. Man, did I used to hate fasting. Sometimes, we'd do a 7-day water fast where we couldn't eat or drink anything but water for those 7 days. Since we were a small church, oftentimes it was all hands on deck, especially for a pastor's kid. Once I surrendered my life to Christ, I was put on the fast track to leadership. I was leading the praise and worship team, leading my Christian rap group, playing instruments, the sound man, preaching and teaching lessons, and showing up early to clean the church, and staying late to lock up. The commitment it took to not only lead in church, but to try to be an example that others could follow by denying my flesh, was no easy feat. I fell short at times, and I made a lot of mistakes. But the on-the-job skills that I learned by becoming a leader to my peers was like none I've ever received before.

Conclusion: The Church Made Me

The church made me have to become disciplined at a young age, but I still had a desire to do what some of my other peers were doing. I was in college and I went to an HBCU. The freedom that you have in college compared to high school is starkly different. I was "grown" now. I didn't have to "ask" for permission. I could go where I want to go and do what I want to do. The only thing was, I got saved at that age. So technically, I couldn't go where I wanted to go and do what I wanted to do. I now had to submit my lifestyle to these Christian disciplines that I opted in for. I had to be set apart.

This was hard, because man, I was in my prime. One of the most difficult practices was abstinence. I had access to all the college fun I wanted and I chose to practice abstinence, to wait until marriage. None of my friends were doing this early on. I had opportunities to go to the college parties and see where the night led to. But I could not do it. I was convicted. Now that I said I was going to live a certain lifestyle, I didn't want to be a hypocrite, so everything that my friends were saying "Yes" to, I had to say "No" to.

The church made me have discipline. It made me be able to deny myself and go against the grain. It made me have the will to say "No" to temporary pleasures, and develop steadfastness when the path that I'd chosen was not the popular one. Do you know how many people around you take the popular path? Most people do what they're told to do. They don't chart their own course. They take the course of least resistance and most accepted. You have to have a strong will to say that I will not take that course. I will take the course that I've paved for myself. And honestly, it's not easy. But the church taught me how to say "No" even when the popular answer was "Yes". This inevitably taught me how to be a leader. The mere fact that I was going a different direction than all of my peers made me a leader. And then once I took that vow, I had to accept the responsibilities that came with it.

Many of my peers thought I was crazy. But you want to know what's even crazier? Most of my peers eventually ended up taking that vow with me. So not only did I become a leader because I chose a different path, I became a leader because that's what the church needed. I learned how to serve. I learned how to sacrifice my desires for a greater mission. I learned how to be driven by something bigger than me. I learned how to keep pushing even when I didn't feel like it, and I learned that a lot of times you have to do what you need to do so that you can eventually get to do what you want to do. A lot of ways that I served in the church wasn't because I had a desire to do them. It was my duty. I wanted to be faithful to the duty bestowed upon me.

I also learned how to become a better communicator and public speaker in church. You know, since our church was small, there were always speaking opportunities. If you attend a small church, most times, they want all of the help they can get. This may cause them to be a little more flexible with speaking opportunities. Sometimes, the pastor was burned out, or sick. I got a chance to hone my speaking gift in church. I learned how to tell stories in a way that connected with the audience, and I got a chance to learn my style of communication after mimicking all of my favorite preachers at one point. After years of speaking, I finally felt comfortable in my own skin, in my own voice. If I had not had the opportunity to exercise this gift in church, I'm not sure I'd be where I am now.

The church is where I became a leader; It's where I developed as a speaker and communicator, and ultimately, the place where I learned how to delay self-gratification.

The church is where I became a leader; It's where I developed as a speaker and communicator, and ultimately, the place where I learned how to delay self-gratification. It's the place where I learned discipline. For you to become who you are born to be, the main thing that you're going to need is discipline. Please, NEVER forget that word. These are all core qualities you need as an individual who's going after a big purpose and vision in your life. You'll need to be able to lead others. You'll need to be able to communicate your vision and get people to buy into it. You'll need to be able to say "No" to things that are gratifying for extended periods of time. These are all character traits that unbeknownst to me, I developed by serving in a small church. Who knew, right?

Premise: The College

When I transitioned to college the second time around, I was coming from a church environment. Initially, I had dropped out of college and started working. This is when I became a christian and started serving in the church. After serving there for a few years, I had the desire to go back to school. So I did, I attended a community college. Going back to college was a little intimidating for me at first. I felt behind and ashamed that I dropped out in the first place. It took me some time to build up the courage to even go back. I felt like I initially missed my opportunity and now, I was too old to go back to college. I laugh at myself when I think about this because actually, I was still very young, still in my twenties. Like I mentioned in previous chapters, attending college the second time around was different. I was more disciplined and more focused. I had a greater grasp on my personal life mission and who I wanted to become and a better idea of how college aligned with my purpose. So this time, I wasn't just attending college because that's what you were supposed to do after graduating high school. I was attending college this time around on a mission.

The college environment was also different this time around. I went to an HBCU my first time going to college, and it was full of distractions for a young lad fresh out of high school. I mean, you had freedom, girls, fraternities, girls, parties, girls...oh yeah, did I forget to mention girls? Lol. Honestly, I was consumed by the freedom and I wasn't focused enough. I needed to mature to be able to handle the enticement of college. But the second time around, I was more focused; not easily swayed, not easily distracted. The first time going to college, it was all about the exciting lifestyle and wanting to experience all that this HBCU experience had to offer. It wasn't about grades and graduating. This time going to college was all about mission, purpose, and alignment. It was all business the second time around. There were no parties, and the campus wasn't buzzing with a lot of activities. You knew you were there to just get to work. I was focused.

The only challenge for me was transitioning from church culture to college culture. The people talked differently, they wore different clothing, and they carried themselves differently. If I wanted to fit in, I had to adapt. College, the second time around, taught me versatility.

Conclusion: College Taught Me

College taught me how to be a chameleon - how to adapt to any environment and become what was necessary to blend in, but also shine at the same time. College taught me how to be versatile. I needed to know how to kick it with my homeboys in a white tee and air forces, but I also needed to know how to properly wear a suit so that people who wouldn't normally give me a conversation would take me seriously. College introduced me to a world of silent world changers. They weren't famous, they didn't have crowds screaming their names, they weren't athletes, but they were closing multi-million, if not billion dollar deals behind closed doors. These were the rooms you wanted to be in and college showed me not only how to get into those rooms, college showed me how to conduct myself once I got into those rooms.

Premise: The Divorce

I've always been the type of man who loved love. I can remember ever since I was young, I was the guy who wanted to be in a relationship. I was the guy who wanted to get married. Since I had become a Christian and I was practicing abstinence at a young age, marriage had become even more of a priority for me, it was high on the priority list. But, I needed to find a viable suitor. So I got married young. I wouldn't try to steer anyone away from getting married young, but I will say that if you're going to get married young, you need mentors, supportive family and friends, a counselor, and more. I know this may sound like a lot but it's true. When you get married young, you don't really know yourself, nor do you really grasp who you are becoming.

When you take on this journey of spending the rest of your life with someone else at a young age, you've decided to take that journey together. It's going to require a lot of love, patience, and compassion. As a young man, I can honestly say that those quality traits are easier to write about than to actually exude. It requires a lot of character development to adequately show love, patience, and compassion to someone. This was something that I was about to learn real soon.

I got married at 21 and my wife at the time was 19. I was young, zealous, prideful, and a know-it-all. I had the gift of gab, so I was already naturally a good talker, and I'm surprised that somewhere down the line I didn't end up being a car sales-man because I sure knew how to convince people to buy into my ideas and philosophies. She had recently graduated high school and came from a broken home where she was raised by a single mother. She also had a lot of trauma happen in her childhood that spilled over into our marriage. How could she or I know that this would be the case at 19-years old? I came from a home where I got to watch my step dad and mom argue for the first two years of their marriage like everyday. They communicated. They talked. But from what I now know, even though they talked, they weren't communicating in a healthy productive way with each other.

Because I witnessed my parents argue so much, I didn't mind arguing with my spouse. I actually thought that it was a sign of "true love". She didn't like to argue, but I did. Can you guess where I may have gotten this idea from? My parents. They argued, but they loved each other. They argued so badly at times I thought it would come to blows. I would go into the kitchen and pick up a pot just in case I heard some tussling. I wasn't going to let my stepdad put his hands on my mom. This was my example of a "good marriage".

I was a communicator, but I still didn't know HOW to communicate. She was an internalizer, so she didn't communicate, she would just shut down. This wasn't a recipe for healthy communication in our marriage. This was a recipe for disaster. I didn't know that I was beating her up with my words at the time. I never called her out of her name or anything like that, but I'm sure I knew how to make her feel low without the need to do so. Because I was so good at talking, when we would have conversations she would just shut down, and that would only make me angrier. You would think that something would have told me, "She's shutting down Josh, maybe you should try a different approach." But nope, I would still keep talking in the tone that would just make her feel worse about herself.

You want to know another thing I never witnessed my step dad do one time in their 20-year marriage? I never witnessed my step dad ever apologize to my mom. So, do you think I ever apologized to my wife at the time? No. If I did it was rare. I felt justified, why apologize? This was a contributing factor to my wife's infidelity. She had just bore our new born son and convinced me to let her go out of town to visit some family in another state. I had huge reservations because we weren't on the same page and were still having problems. Something didn't feel right about it but nevertheless, I granted her wishes. Once she was a thousand miles away, this is when I found out that she was having an affair and told me that she was leaving me. She wanted a divorce. This truly broke me at the time. I didn't want to lose my family. This is where I learned compassion.

Conclusion: Divorce Taught Me

Divorce taught me compassion. I realized that compassion was easier to show when the person on the receiving end of your compassion deserved your patience and empathy. But what if you felt like they didn't deserve it. What if they wronged you? What if they betrayed you? What if they talked down to you and treated you like trash? Did they deserve your compassion then? When she initially left and told me that she wanted a divorce after admitting to an affair, I was livid. I quoted every scripture about infidelity and justified my anger. I demanded that she repent and come back home. But that was only pushing her further away. I wasn't compassionate, I didn't even know what it looked like to show true compassion towards someone who had betrayed you. Why would someone who betrays you even deserve compassion? If we're honest, when we are betrayed, most of us feel like the person who committed the transgression deserves punishment, not compassion, not empathy. The only way that I had gotten my wife back was by showing her compassion and empathizing with her.

This affected me in so many other areas in my life because I didn't realize how empathetic I was to people. I had it rough growing up. I felt like I needed compassion and empathy but did I get it? No. If I didn't get compassion, why should I have to show it to others? If I seemed to turn out to be a good young man, why couldn't they? But how could I ever lead people without compassion? How could I ever truly care about the people serving my vision if I wasn't compassionate towards them? If I treated them like objects who were just there to do a job, why would I expect them to stick around for years? God knew that I needed to learn how to be compassionate and he used my marriage as my classroom.

Needlesstosay, we still went through a divorce, and that was one of the darkest, most embarrassing times of my life. People talked about me, sneered, blamed me without knowing the whole story, and villainized me while making her the victim. Maturity taught me to look at myself in the mirror before pointing the finger, so that's why I only gave you guys a snippet of the story because I had taken accountability for how my actions contributed to my divorce. But trust me, it was more than that. And I definitely wasn't the villain. Neither of us were, we were just young.

Going through that divorce humbled me because of how embarrassing it was. I told myself that I would NEVER get divorced, and here I am, standing before a judge, asking her to grant my divorce petition. I felt like a failure. And truth be told, I did fail. But failure doesn't have to be final. Though my marriage didn't make it, I learned so many things that I was dedicated to becoming a better man. Remember what I told you in the previous chapter, everything that happened to you happened for you. Though I never wanted to go through a divorce, looking back on it, I do realize how it contributed to making me more resilient, better, and wiser for my next wife.

You Were Born For This

There is a reason why I gave you brief examples of points in my life. I wanted you to see how much I learned from every part of my life. Look, there are many more examples that I could have given you, but that in and of itself would have taken me another book. I want you to know that everything in your life is meant to work out for your good, even the bad things. As I write this, I can think of some of the most horrible, despicable situations that people have been through; from being molested and raped, and even sex trafficked. I can hear the reader who's been through terrible things like this ask, "So you're telling me those situations were for my good?" No, I'm not saying that. That horrible circumstance should have never happened to you. I don't wish these kinds of abominable situations on anyone. But that still doesn't change the fact that it's still a part of your story.

Will you continue to let your shame overshadow your story? Are you only the shame that you experienced from the embarrassment of your story?

Will you continue to let your shame overshadow your story? Are you only the shame that you experienced from the embarrassment of your story? I believe that you are not. Yes, you were the victim, but you don't have to continue to be.

Even though you didn't have a choice in some of the things that happened to you, you do have a choice to forgive and not be shackled by shame, guilt, and revenge. That's your choice. Don't allow that horrible situation to rob you of your choice to thrive, heal, and move forward.

That's what I want for you. I want you to choose power. I want you to accept every situation in your life and let it empower you to become who you were born to be. There are evil people out there. You didn't have a choice in some of the things that transpired in your life. But if you're honest, there are some decisions you made that you weren't forced into. Accept that these were just bad decisions because bad decisions come with this life. Even in the midst of your bad decisions, I want you to choose to let those decisions empower you, not keep you in chains. I'll admit, it's difficult to see the beauty in a lot of terrible things that happen in this life. Both of my heroes, my dads, passed away within 3 years of each other. Both were pastors, and passed away from sickness. Can you imagine how this rocked my faith? I grew up in a pentecostal church that told me if you had enough faith, God would heal you from any disease.

Yet, there I was watching my fathers wither away. If I'm honest, it's hard for me to see the beauty in those losses. If you ask me, I'd rather them be here than be gone. But what if I stayed in that place of anger and sadness, how would that benefit me? Would it benefit me at all? Most likely not. I would still have immeasurable resentment built up towards God for killing my dads. At least that's how I used to see it.

I was unhappy when I was in this state. I couldn't move forward because I was filled with bitterness and hate. It kept me stuck and stagnant. But even though watching them lose weight and eventually die were some of the most challenging moments of my life, there was beauty in it. Their passing made me ask myself, "Who am I?" "Why am I here?" "Do I really believe what I say that I believe?" Their passing on was life-defining for me. And I know that they would have wanted me to give life all that I had. I know that they wouldn't have wanted me to live empty, not full of potential. Their words still live on in my heart and motivate me to this day.

...even in the most tragic situations, if you allow it, you can find the beauty in them too.

So why am I saying this? Because even in the most tragic situations, if you allow it, you can find the beauty in them too. Everything you've been through is a culmination of moments and experiences to propel you into your purpose. Without the uniqueness of those experiences, you would not have become who you are today. You can chart your own course. You can change the trajectory of your future. You can become who you were meant to be. It all starts with a decision. Continue to let the chains of fear restrain you, hold you back, and keep you hidden in a dungeon; or break free from your chains of fear and boldly accept your calling. The choice is up to YOU. But if you ask me, there's one thing that I know for sure. No one, and I mean NO ONE can do what you've been put on this earth to do, because you were fearfully and wonderfully made.

You, my friend...were Born For This!

ACKNOWLEDGEMENTS

Thank you to both my dads and my mom for giving me the spiritual foundation, and teaching me what it is to live like a man of integrity.

Thank you number 7 for encouraging, supporting, and challenging me every step of the way, your support has been invaluable.

Thank you Johnny Gentry for being the transparent honest mentor that I've always needed.

I'd like to thank my entire family who has been a support system and a deep sense of motivation for me from the beginning.

I'm thankful for all of my close friends who have rocked with me, served with me, and sacrificed with me. Without you, this would have not been possible.

I'm thankful to all my fans and supporters. Every inbox, email, dm, and word of encouragement gave me the push to keep going when I thought to myself "what's the point?". Your belief in me has been like water on a hot day.

I'd also like to thank my non-supporters(haters). I know you're watching and spectating from the bleachers. Cheers to you ;)

Thank you, reader, for reading this book and believing that something said could ignite your passion for the next phase of your life from the inside out.

Most importantly, Thank You God. What can I say? You always kept the same energy. You never left me nor forsake me. Your love sometimes is incomprehensible, I'm extremely grateful for it.

About The Author

Joshua is the recipient of the Volunteer Service Award by President Barack Obama and has been featured on networks such as BET, Vice, Fox, The Shade Room and more. He's been inspiring thousands through speaking and content for over 10 years and has spoken to millions through platforms he's graced. To learn more visit joshuadillard.com.

HOW CAN WE HELP YOUR ORGANIZATION?

Looking to inspire your congregation, students, or audience through humor, story-telling, and authenticity? Or would you like to engage your staff, employees, or leadership in a way that creates a healthy company culture, increases overall productivity, and builds more buy-in for your business?

Learn how we can bring lasting impact to your college, church, or business by visiting **JoshuaDillard.com**.

CPSIA information can be obtained
at www.ICGtesting.com
Printed in the USA
BVHW031926060323
659767BV00025B/382/J